what do we know and what should we do about...?

tax justice

what do we
know and
what should we
do about...?

tax justice

Alex Cobham

S Sage

1 Oliver's Yard
55 City Road
London EC1Y 1SP

2455 Teller Road
Thousand Oaks
California 91320

Unit No. 323–333, Third Floor, F-Block
International Trade Tower, Nehru Place
New Delhi 110 019

8 Marina View Suite 43-053
Asia Square Tower 1
Singapore 018960

Editor: Michael Ainsley
Editorial assistant: Sarah Moorhouse
Production editor: Imogen Roome
Copyeditor: Clare Weaver
Proofreader: Neil Dowden
Marketing manager: Fauzia Eastwood
Cover design: Wendy Scott
Typeset by: C&M Digitals (P) Ltd, Chennai, India
Printed in the UK

Library of Congress Control Number: 2023946661

British Library Cataloguing in Publication data

A catalogue record for this book is available from the British Library

ISBN 978-1-5296-6777-6
ISBN 978-1-5296-6776-9 (pbk)

At Sage we take sustainability seriously. Most of our products are printed in the UK using responsibly sourced papers and boards. When we print overseas we ensure sustainable papers are used as measured by the Paper Chain Project grading system. We undertake an annual audit to monitor our sustainability.

For Catherine and David, y por Pino y José

contents

About the series   ix
About the author   xi
Acknowledgements   xiii

1   **Introduction**   1
    The 4 Rs of tax   3
    Tax is our social superpower   10
    Outline   15

2   **Background**   19

3   **What do we know about tax justice?**   27
    Perspectives on tax justice   28
    The scale of tax injustice   37
    Definitional questions: Tax abuse, avoidance and evasion 38
    Offshore tax evasion   42
    Multinational tax abuse   53
    Harms and history   63

4   **What should we do about tax justice?**   71
    The ABC of tax transparency   72
    Domestic measures   88
    International and institutional measures   102

5   **Conclusion**   109

References   115
Index   133

about the series

Every news bulletin carries stories which relate in some way to the social sciences – most obviously politics, economics and sociology, but also, often, anthropology, business studies, security studies, criminology, geography and many others.

Yet despite the existence of large numbers of academics who research these subjects, relatively little of their work is known to the general public.

There are many reasons for that, but, arguably, it is that the kinds of formats that social scientists publish in, and the way in which they write, are simply not accessible to the general public.

The guiding theme of this series is to provide a format and a way of writing which addresses this problem. Each book in the series is concerned with a topic of widespread public interest, and each is written in a way which is readily understandable to the general reader with no particular background knowledge.

The authors are academics with an established reputation and a track record of research in the relevant subject. They provide an overview of the research knowledge about the subject, whether this be long-established or reporting the most recent findings, widely accepted or still controversial. Often in public debate there is a demand for greater clarity about the facts, and that is one of the things the books in this series provide.

However, in social sciences, facts are often disputed and subject to different interpretations. They do not always, or even often, 'speak for themselves'. The authors therefore strive to show the different interpretations or the key controversies about their topics, but without getting bogged down in arcane academic arguments.

Not only can there be disputes about facts but also there are almost invariably different views on what should follow from these facts. And, in any case, public debate requires more of academics than just to report facts; it is also necessary to make suggestions and recommendations about the implications of these facts.

Thus each volume also contains ideas about 'what we should do' within each topic area. These are based upon the authors' knowledge of the field but also, inevitably, upon their own views, values and preferences. Readers may not agree with them, but the intention is to provoke thought and well-informed debate.

Chris Grey, Series Editor
Professor of Organization Studies
Royal Holloway, University of London

about the author

Alex Cobham is an economist and chief executive of Tax Justice Network. Alex is also a commissioner for the Scottish government's Poverty and Inequality Commission, and a member of the steering group for the Independent Commission for the Reform of International Corporate Taxation (ICRICT). He previously worked at Oxford University, Christian Aid, Save the Children and the Center for Global Development, and has consulted for a range of UN bodies and the World Bank. Alex's research has focused on inequalities within and between countries, and on the scale of international tax abuse and other illicit financial flows. Previous books include *The Uncounted* (Polity Press) and *Estimating Illicit Financial Flows* (Oxford University Press, with Petr Janský). His website is http://uncounted.org.

acknowledgements

This book would not exist without the efforts of a great many other people – those who have built and are building the global tax justice movement; and those whose care and support has enabled my writing. I'm grateful to Michael Ainsley for suggesting the book and for his careful and constructive engagement on the text.

Among the builders, I'm especially grateful to those who act in grace and solidarity, without ego. Happily, there are many. Dereje Alemayehu, Gurminder Bhambra, Gamal Ibrahim, Bernadette O'Hare, Irene Ovonji-Odida, Rakesh Rajani and Tove Ryding deserve particular thanks.

I'm grateful to colleagues and board members at the Tax Justice Network: as builders of the movement; for their support for this book; and above all for the love and care that the team has shown each other through the turbulence of the last years.

I thank the excellent secretariat and members of the Scottish government's Poverty and Inequality Commission, including the tax working group, those who provided evidence to us, and the Experts by Experience Panel, from whom it has been a privilege to learn.

And I'm indebted, as ever, to MAP – on whom I can always rely to be guided towards what is truly important.

introduction

In 2021, 5 million children died before turning 5 years old. Many of these tragedies occurred because children were deprived of their basic right to quality health care, vaccinations, proper food and clean water and sanitation.

UNICEF, 2023

Countries are on course to lose nearly US$5 trillion in tax to multinational corporations and wealthy individuals using tax havens to underpay tax over the next 10 years. The future losses of public money would be equivalent to losing a year of worldwide spending on public health.

Tax Justice Network, 2023

They say death and taxes are the only two certain things in life. One thing we do know for sure: the lack of tax justice leads to unnecessary deaths. And more broadly, it leaves us all with poorer, nastier, shorter, more brutal and solitary lives – as the 17th-century political philosopher Thomas Hobbes might have put it.

The global COVID-19 pandemic offers a harsh reminder of the importanoc of effective government. The first wave required urgent, coordinated policy responses including what was, for many countries, a generationally unprecedented societal shift in behaviour. Our mutual interdependence was made clear, as was the critical role of the state – most obviously through the provision of public health services.

Public health is the most basic sphere of government action. Where it works well, it is treasured. The UK's National Health Service (NHS) has until recently been seen as one of the country's greatest achievements. Even with record dissatisfaction with NHS performance (Morris et al., 2023), over three-quarters of people supported the statement 'The NHS is crucial to British society and we must do everything to maintain it' (Health Foundation, 2022). Almost the same number (71%) supported greater government spending. There could hardly be a more obvious case than public health for the benefits of collective action. Members of a community agree to pool resources as a joint response to the possibility, or rather the inevitability, that they and their loved ones will require medical care in future.

Tax is the mechanism by which that pooling can be universal, intergenerational and unconditional. The needless mortality associated with underfunded public health systems – not only in the UK but around the world – is the most obvious symptom of tax *in*justice.

Estimates vary, but cross-border tax abuse is likely to account for around half a trillion dollars of lost revenue around the world each year (see survey chapters in Cobham & Janský, 2020). And the revenue losses are the tip of the iceberg. Underlying them are illicit flows of covertly shifted profits and hidden incomes, of many trillions of dollars a year. That makes tax abuse a materially significant distortion in the world's economic accounts. In other words, what people hide in order not to pay taxes is big enough to put question marks over our understanding of the whole global economy.

The distribution of the resulting tax losses tells a story. The State of Tax Justice 2023 (Tax Justice Network, 2023) confirms previous findings that the largest absolute losses are suffered by the largest economies including the US (US$177 billion), UK ($45 billion) and France ($33 billion). But the largest *relative* losses, by far, occur in countries with lower per capita incomes. For the US, UK and France, the losses are in the range of 10% to 20% of public health spending. For many countries, that figure rises to 30% or even 50% of their public health spending. For some, including India and Zambia, the losses exceed the *total* spent on public health.

As explored further in the next section, research shows that reversing those losses would likely have saved the lives of six hundred thousand children under five over a ten-year period (Nelson, 2021). It's not just that tax abuse screws up our understanding of the economy. That hardly matters, compared to the damage to people.

As an aside: that damage is the reason I'm writing this, and I'm far from neutral. I began my professional career as a researcher at the University of Oxford at the tail end of the 1990s, where I was lucky enough to become involved in some of the early work then on the damage done by tax abuse. Over the years I've moved between roles with varying emphases on research and advocacy, but always aiming to overturn the neglect of tax as an instrument for sustainable human development – in countries at all levels of per capita income.

Since 2016 I've had the privilege to be the chief executive of the Tax Justice Network, which receives the proceeds of this book. The views here are mine, rather than necessarily those of the organisation. We do though have a shared belief: that our tax and financial systems are our most powerful tools for creating a just society that gives equal weight to the needs of everyone. This view of tax *justice* emerges, along with a range of policy proposals, from the decades of international, academic and other research and analysis which is surveyed here.

The 4 Rs of tax

The 4 Rs of tax (Cobham, 2005; Nelson, 2021) are four significant contributions to social progress which effective taxation can deliver, and provide a simple framework that I refer to throughout this book. The potential for tax to contribute to reparative justice has seen a 5th R proposed, and this is discussed in a later chapter.

Revenue

Revenue is the first of the 4 Rs. Lack of actual cash is rarely a binding constraint on governments, which can generally print money and can usually borrow from financial institutions. But the value of money that governments print and the ability of governments to borrow ultimately depend on the credibility of the government in question. That in turn rests, ultimately, on the belief that governments can and will raise revenue.

Directly and indirectly, then, it is governments' ability to raise revenue that underpins the ability to fund public services and administration. Some governments can obtain revenue from overseas aid (that is, grants from other countries), and from the proceeds of a country's natural resources. Dependency on these sources create their own issues, however (see 'Representation' below).

Taxation provides the only sustainable revenue source fully consistent with independent sovereignty. Revenue losses due to tax abuse therefore hinder inclusive spending on the likes of health and education, and all their potential benefits.

These benefits are the focus of the GRADE model (Government Revenue and Development Estimations) developed at the University of St Andrews. The model shows the extent to which countries are likely to achieve improved health outcomes and other fundamental economic and social rights as they increase government revenues.

From a panel of data covering almost all countries of the world, Hall et al. (2021) identify a non-linear relationship between additional revenues and improved health outcomes. Specifically, the benefits of additional revenue translate much more powerfully into health benefits for countries with lower revenue as a starting point. They find, for example, that 'a 10% increase in per-capita government revenue in Afghanistan in 2002 ($24.49 million) is associated with a reduction in the under-5 mortality rate by 12.35 deaths per 1000 births and 13,094 lives saved [and] a decrease in the maternal mortality ratio of 9.3 deaths per 100,000 live births and 99 maternal deaths averted' (p. 213).

The GRADE model has been applied to estimates of revenue losses due to cross-border tax abuse by multinational companies and by individuals with hidden offshore wealth. Assessing the gains for countries with data availability over a ten-year period reveals the following numbers of people potentially accessing their fundamental human rights. Access to sanitation: 34 million people; access to drinking water: 17 million people; additional year of schooling: 3 million children; and additional survivors of child mortality: 600,000 children, and maternal mortality: 73,000 mothers (Nelson, 2021, drawing on O'Hare et al., 2022).

For countries with much higher levels of revenue per capita, including the UK, the relationship to health outcomes is less dramatic – but not necessarily less clear. The King's Fund, a respected health think tank, recently published a major report entitled 'The rise and decline of the NHS in England 2000–20: How political failure led to the crisis in the NHS and social care' (Ham, 2023). There is no mystery either to the rise ('Multi-year funding increases above the long-term average and a series of reforms resulted in major improvements in NHS performance between 2000 and 2010') or the decline ('Performance has declined since 2010 as a result of much lower funding increases, limited funds for capital investment', p. 2). Nor are the impacts in doubt, with 'growing evidence that health inequalities are widening and life expectancy is stalling' (Marmot et al., 2020).

Successive decisions to underfund the NHS have been political rather than financial, in the sense that no government of the period faced a binding revenue constraint. But the justifying arguments were consistently based on claims that fiscal pressures required national 'austerity'. While austerity arguments were commonly used by high-income country governments after the financial crisis that began in 2008–2009, UK governments were uniquely extreme in their approach. Rather than combining spending cuts and tax rises, the UK cut *taxes* and then imposed much harsher spending reductions than would have been required (Cobham, 2016). The 2010s joined the 1980s as the only periods of the NHS's existence that have seen sustained reductions in its funding as a share of GDP (Harker, 2019).

Redistribution

While hugely important, lost revenue and forgone expenditure is only one part of the damage done when tax justice is absent. The second R of tax is redistribution. Tax has a fundamental role to play in challenging inequalities, by ensuring that those with the highest incomes and wealth make a progressively higher contribution. Coupled with inclusive public spending, the overall redistribution can be substantial.

Tax abuse also defeats redistribution. A variety of evidence points to the same conclusion, as Chapter 3 explores in more detail. Tax abuse is heavily concentrated in the households with the highest levels of income and wealth (e.g. Alstadsæter et al., 2019; Guyton et al., 2021) and the largest multinational companies (e.g. Garcia-Bernardo & Janský, 2023). The effect is that those most able to contribute more very often contribute less. The highest marginal tax rates in practice can fall on low- and middle-income households, while smaller and domestic business face an uneven playing field because larger, multinational competitors enjoy a relative tax subsidy.

The indirect effects may be stronger. The well-supported fear of tax abuse by elites often provides the basis to argue for lower tax rates. That impetus for the 'race to the bottom' degrades the degree of progressivity in the tax system on paper, even before those at the top end of the distribution seek to dodge their responsibilities. Lobbying by elite groups often weakens progressive taxation and distorts the overall system, as well as creating specific loopholes in order to reduce their contribution (Fastenrath et al., 2022; Lin, 2021; Meade & Li, 2015; Richter et al., 2009).

The failure of redistribution through tax can be pivotal to societies' failure to address the most glaring inequalities – typically the overlapping inequalities that include women, racialised and other marginalised groups, and disabled people. Tax justice is a key tool for human rights, including women's rights (ACIJ et al., 2021; Nelson, 2021).

Repricing

The third R of tax reflects the extent to which the tax system can contribute to social aims through the repricing of public goods and public 'bads'. By varying the tax rate on economic activities with major public health implications, say, from tobacco consumption to carbon emissions, an effective tax system can support significant shifts.

Taxing better would help to save the planet. Social outcomes are inevitably worse where tax systems cannot effectively reprice public goods and bads.

Tobacco taxation provides a relatively simple example. Private consumption of tobacco by individuals has broader social impacts. First, the individual in question increases their own health risks, from cancers to cardiac issues. That has social implications for the future public cost of their care. In addition, the *smoking* of tobacco increases the health risks of a multitude of people who are also exposed, again with broader social implications.

There is a strong evidence base that specific tobacco taxes can both reduce the level of consumption and harms done, and also raise revenues to offset the public costs. In addition, and in part because the harms of tobacco consumption are disproportionately borne by lower-income households and marginalised groups, tobacco taxes are highly progressive (Tobacconomics & STOP, 2023). Without an effective tax system in place, however, these gains cannot be achieved. 'Effective' in this case, and more generally, includes being able to resist the highly funded and targeted counter-lobbying (see e.g. Russ et al., 2022; Smith et al., 2013; Tax Justice Network, 2017; Zatonski et al., 2023).

Equivalent arguments can be constructed for the social costs of particular products and services in many other industries, including high-sugar drinks and highly processed foods, alcohol and breast milk substitutes. The existence of a 'finance curse' (Christensen et al., 2016; Shaxson, 2011) – whereby an excessively large financial services sector imposes a range of social and economic costs on a country, distorting the balance of economic activity, increasing inequalities, and in the extreme undermining democratic processes – similarly provides a rationale for repricing in order to reduce the private returns to the sector.

A broader, and vital application relates to carbon emissions. As with tobacco, raising the cost of emissions-intensive industries can both reduce emissions and raise revenues to tackle the resulting harms. Damage to the planet is so advanced, however, that survival is likely to require blunter measures such as banning all new fossil fuel extraction. But repricing can still play a role in ensuring that remaining emissions are reduced, and – perhaps more importantly – providing the basis for revenues to flow to countries and populations with the least historic responsibility, and the greatest current vulnerability (Mager & Chaparro, 2023). Current proposals risk raising revenues in high-income countries, harming industries in lower-income countries, and likely failing to reduce emissions (e.g. He et al., 2022; Ülgen, 2023).

Lastly, repricing also provides opportunities to pursue other social and economic policy aims. Raising marginal tax rates on top incomes, for example, need not to be intended to generate significant revenue. Very high rates make it increasingly expensive for employers to pay the highest salaries and send a signal that such salaries are not socially preferred. This can lead to reduced inequality, with all the public health and social benefits that entails (e.g. Marmot et al., 2020) – even without direct redistribution.

Representation

The fourth R of tax, often overlooked, may well be the most important: political representation. Tax is the 'glue' in the social contract. In paying tax, we develop and commit to a common relationship, in which government is not some remote 'other', but fundamentally is *of* us.

We pay tax, and feel we have a stake in our government's spending and other decisions. That feeling leads us to hold government accountable. And over time, governments that depend more on tax should tend to *be* more accountable. They should spend more inclusively for the benefit of all in society; and they should become less prone to corruption.

The evidence supports this view. The share of tax in government spending turns out to be one of the only things that is systematically associated with improvements in political representation and governance

(Prichard et al., 2018). The result appears strongest with respect to direct taxes – those on incomes, profits and capital, which also tend to be the most salient, or noticeable to taxpayers compared to, for example, consumption taxes such as VAT (value-added tax). Where governments depend more heavily on tax revenue, the need to maintain public support for spending decisions is greater, and over time accountability increases and democratic processes are strengthened.

In contrast, when governments are able to rely more on natural resource wealth, borrowing or foreign aid, greater reliance on non-tax revenue is associated with weaker democracy and sharply lower likelihood of a country transitioning *to* democracy. Governments with low tax dependence are much more easily able to resist political opposition, including through repression. In analysis covering two centuries of data, researchers at the UN University's World Institute for Development Economics Research (UNU-WIDER) demonstrate a long-run relationship between judicial or legislative constraints on the executive power of government, and tax revenues – with direct taxes being the key element (Savoia et al., 2023). Governments that depend more on tax are less likely to act repressively. Conversely, a public that feels less strongly that government is spending *their* money is less likely to demand accountability for spending decisions, and corruption and misgovernance becomes more likely.

In the long term, this 4th R is likely to be the most important channel by which tax can support our collective well-being. Higher tax revenues are associated with higher public health expenditure, unsurprisingly; and higher public health expenditures are associated with better public health outcomes. And research suggests a multiplier effect that goes well beyond the availability of revenue (Carter & Cobham, 2016; Reeves et al., 2015).

For a given level of overall public spending, governments that are more reliant on direct taxes tend to spend a higher share on public health. There is evidence too of a positive association between reliance on direct taxes, and the coverage of the public health system. Even holding spending constant, it seems that more of the public are likely to be included in a public health system that derives a greater share of its funding from direct taxes. In other words, it is not just revenue or spending that matters. Public health outcomes may be better, for the same cost, simply because the source of funds is (direct) tax.

Further research from the GRADE team adds to the case. They extend their examination of direct impacts of revenue losses to consider the intermediating role of governance, and confirm virtuous links: additional revenues have stronger benefits on outcomes such as child mortality, when states are better governed; while additional revenues, including from tax, also improve governance over time, further strengthening human outcomes (Hall & O'Hare, 2022).

Tax is our social superpower

Taken together, the 4 Rs show why we should think about our ability to tax as a *social superpower*. When we organise ourselves in this way, we create the potential for a state that has both the ability and the accountability to support progress for us all.

Media attention is still often given to 'small state' rhetoric. This idea was perhaps most clearly stated by 'The Great Communicator', US president Ronald Reagan in his farewell speech in 1989: 'Man is not free unless government is limited... As government expands, liberty contracts.' Underpinning this libertarian view is the idea that the state is an obstacle to human progress rather than a helpful or even necessary form of organising ourselves for the common good.

The historian of ideas Quinn Slobodian has traced in his book *Crack-Up Capitalism: Market Radicals and the Dream of a World Without Democracy* (2023) how such libertarian views continue to echo around the globe, as wealthy backers fund lobbying to create political spaces – from freeports and tax havens to 'charter cities' – where taxation, regulation and human rights need not impinge upon the ideal of 'freedom'.

But the evidence is strong that the public – in country after country – is committed to the social contract, and the view that states act on our behalf and should be accountable to us.

Polling for the Fairness Foundation (2023) shows a remarkably strong national consensus in the UK, across supporters of all political parties, for a stronger state role delivering on a broad social contract. Polling across African countries by Afrobarometer (Afrobarometer, 2023; Isbell, 2022) shows consistent growth in public demands for state accountability, and growing majorities who believe that taxes must be more progressive.

Other sources of government funding can be used as part of a balanced strategy, from aid and natural resource wealth to debt and money creation. Only tax, however, is fully sustainable and consistent with independent, sovereign and representative policymaking over the long term. Only for tax do the benefits *increase* with greater reliance – whereas reliance on each other source ultimately increases the risks of corruption and misgovernance, of uncontrolled inflation, of exhausting natural resources or of contributing to irreversible planetary damage.

If tax is our superpower, where does *justice* enter the discussion? Is it not simply a question of ensuring the *effectiveness* of tax, and the job is done?

There is a pervasive tendency, in national and international policy processes, to frame tax as highly technical. That labelling performs two functions. First, it strengthens the gatekeeping role of tax professionals. That supports the disproportionate influence over tax policy in many countries of the major accounting firms and law firms. It also reinforces the revolving door system by which tax professionals from those firms and major multinationals move in and out of employment with finance ministries and international tax bodies (see, e.g., Christensen, 2021; Christensen et al., 2022; and Drucker & Hakim, 2021).

Second, this approach also conflicts with the fact that tax – in its administration, as well as the chosen policies – is fundamentally political. The decisions taken, and not taken, cannot be reduced to mere technical questions (however much lobbyists for particular interests might seek to present things in this way).

For example, it is common to see corporate tax policy decisions framed by think tanks and lobbyists in terms of a trade-off, between higher tax rates or higher investment (e.g. Adam et al., 2022; Devereux, 2021; Zuluaga, 2016). This tends to require a possible respondent to demonstrate an ability to engage with the econometric literature on this highly researched but at best complex and uncertain relationship (Hunady & Orviska, 2014, for example, find 'no statistically significant effect of corporate taxes on FDI', p. 243). The approach also shifts the debate to a negative framing. The implied question becomes: how much can we afford to tax companies, without harming investment, employment and growth?

In practice, corporate tax is likely the least distortionary tax we have, and consistent research findings – even from the likes of the consultancy McKinsey's, or the International Monetary Fund, as Tax Justice Network (2015) surveys – show that tax is simply not a first-order consideration for businesses deciding where to invest. Moreover, corporate income tax plays an important role as a backstop for personal income tax and therefore for the progressive potential of the whole tax system – as otherwise personal income is converted to corporate income (World Bank, 2022).

And the results are now in from a comprehensive meta-analysis of the many studies that have sought to address the ideological claim that corporate tax cuts can drive economic growth. Gechert and Heimberger (2022) find: 'we cannot reject the hypothesis of a zero effect of corporate taxes on growth.' In fact, 'Our results suggest that the prominent role given to corporate tax cuts in policy debates is exaggerated. Tax cuts have certainly stimulated international tax competition in recent decades, but they do not seem to have enhanced growth' (Heimberger & Gechert, 2021).

Even if economic growth was your aim – rather than, say, human well-being – corporate tax cuts don't help.

Ultimately, tax is concerned with distribution. What level of public services do we wish for? What proportion of the profits extracted from a society should private individuals be entitled to keep for themselves? What share should a state retain in order to pay for or reinvest in the factors that made the profit possible in the first place: from the basics of infrastructure and administration like roads, ports and a functioning bureaucracy and legal system, to the more complex features of a healthy human society including those that give rise to fair markets and a highly skilled workforce? What resulting level and types of inequalities are desirable, or acceptable?

This type of question can be all too easily overlooked when tax is pigeonholed as a niche issue for professionals only, or 'too technical' for the rest of society to get involved with. The persistent risk is that we end up with policies that may be technically effective on a particular narrow framing, but are also socially damaging.

For this reason, insisting on the political nature of tax decisions has been a central element of the international tax justice movement that has coalesced and grown over the last two decades.

Few people are ever overjoyed about paying tax. But it's because we notice it, and even resent it, that we feel empowered to demand better from government. The salience of tax matters. We *need* to notice it, for us to obtain the full benefits of this social superpower.

Individual governments have different incentives. Rather than increase the salience of taxes paid, there's a temptation to hide them. Income taxes, for example, are visible as a reduction from the monthly pay slip. Consumption taxes like VAT are much less obvious. They tend, too, to get mixed up with the pricing decisions of shops and suppliers.

With a short-term electoral horizon, policymakers can be drawn towards the least salient taxes. You can see this play out over decades with politicians in the UK as elsewhere being drawn to VAT and preferring 'National Insurance' rises rather than owning an outright increase in personal income tax. (The less obvious nature of NI aside, the major practical difference is of course that NI falls much less progressively across the income distribution – and so like VAT this ends up being regressive too.) A favourite example from the research literature is the finding that Italian mayors who face a tougher contest to be re-elected tend systematically to switch towards the least salient of the revenue-raising instruments that they control – which tend to be fees for government services, as opposed to the more salient property taxes (Bracco et al., 2019).

In a vicious cycle, those incentives for policymakers can also undermine the contribution that tax makes.

It turns out that we all pay more tax than a simple-minded economic analysis would suggest we should. The foundational economic model (Allingham & Sandmo, 1972), assumes that taxpayers will decide whether to comply according to a simple maximisation. The tax rate to be paid, the chances of being caught if you don't, and the penalties that would bring, are then the key factors. But most subsequent research has been based on the fact that this model does not work in practice: that is, people in general are much more compliant than the model would ever predict (e.g. Alm et al., 1992).

Paying tax, the research shows, really is a social act: something we do for more complex reasons including to participate in our communities, rather than out of expectation for a direct return. But our willingness to do this – our tax morale – depends on some key beliefs. We are more likely to comply when when we think everyone else is participating fairly too (Frey & Torgler, 2007). And we comply more fully when we have concern for others and think government is redistributing our contributions well (Alm, 2019).

Short-termist governments may emphasise less progressive taxes like VAT instead of more salient income and wealth taxes. They may also limit the resources for tax authorities to pursue abuse, by major companies at high-income households. And they may introduce tax breaks and loop-holes for major taxpayers (and/or for major donors). In the medium and longer term, such decisions undermine tax morale across the board.

The richest don't pay. So why should I? The system doesn't help those who need it. Why should I contribute? And as that thread unravels, people's sense of a stake in government, and even in society, can weaken.

A virtuous cycle is also possible. Think of a far-sighted government pushing ahead with more progressive taxes, despite the political risks. The salience of these decisions does not improve immediate polling numbers. It does though lead over time to greater accountability and more effective political representation, and ultimately to better social outcomes, from health to broader aspects of human well-being.

The fact that this dynamic can tip either way – and that the incentives generated by our democratic systems may be largely unhelpful – under-scores the importance of recognising that tax is primarily political rather than technical.

The tax contributions we make, and the distributions across society that follow, create what the sociologist and decolonial thinker Gurminder Bhambra refers to (e.g. 2022), following Martin et al. (2009), as a 'web of generalised reciprocity'. Participating in these relationships strengthens the social contract. Or perhaps we should say that these relations *are* the social contract – the give and take of living in, and as, a society.

Such relationships are put at risk when there is a disconnect between the populations participating in taxation and in the distribution of benefits. When some who earn substantial incomes from a society are able to engineer an escape from their contributions, the relationships fail. Most commonly, this occurs through the shifting of corporate profits by multinationals, away from the economy where the profits arose; and by the use of other jurisdictions to hide individuals' ownership of assets and income streams.

If tax is society's superpower, this type of abuse is its kryptonite – along with the special interest lobbying that makes it technically legal, or prevents the effective enforcement of the laws that should stop it.

The first and best thing we can do to inoculate ourselves is to make sure that we understand the importance of tax. That doesn't mean we all need to learn the technical details. And it certainly doesn't mean we all need to agree – quite the opposite. What we want our tax system to deliver should be the subject of vigorous and informed political debate.

That debate is where ideas of tax *justice* can crystallise and inform decision-making. It is also where the threat of tax abuse can be challenged, and where those responsible – including in governments – can be held accountable.

Outline

In this short book I aim to provide a guided tour of the issues and evidence. The following 'Background' chapter extends the discussion of the role of tax in societies, from underlying theories to recent evidence.

That provides context for the chapter 'What do we know about tax justice?'. Here, I explore different perspectives on tax justice, and identify the main elements of broad consensus. The core component is the nature and impact of cross-border tax abuse, including the role of profit shifting by multinational companies, and the exploitation of anonymous, offshore ownership structures. A major driver is the race to the bottom between jurisdictions, in terms of tax and financial (de)regulation. The leading actors, aside from policymakers themselves, are the various professional enablers of tax abuse – including banks, lawyers and major accounting firms.

The cross-border tax abuse in our current period of globalisation is not a purely modern phenomenon. That is, tax abuse is not an anomaly of our time. But nor has it been a constant through the centuries. We can better understand the current period as the third of three imperial ages of illicit financial flows. Each of the three ages is markedly different, although they share common elements. Cumulatively, they have shaped the tax injustice experienced today in countries from the UK to Malawi, from India to Colombia, and from Singapore to Barbados.

A key conclusion to emerge here is that the international nature of the problem means that international coordination is badly needed. That does not mean national governments are powerless, however. There is much that can still be delivered unilaterally or in regional groupings. Continued progress in these areas is almost certainly essential to move forward the global changes that are needed.

In the chapter 'What should we do about tax justice?', I take a critical look at a broad range of proposals to address tax injustice, both unilateral and multilateral. In the last decade in particular, political space has opened up for a range of international measures – many of which were once written off as unrealistic. But there is still far to travel before these are delivered in a way that will powerfully curb tax abuse. At the national level, including in the UK, there remains a lack of understanding and consensus on some core minimum features that should form part of a good tax system. In addition, new quantitative approaches using data on bilateral flows of trade and investment have allowed a more granular analysis of the particular risks and vulnerabilities that individual countries face, and these are yet to be fully exploited. For example, law enforcement and tax authorities can gain much by understanding the main secrecy jurisdictions that are used to hold property in London, say, or the main profit shifting jurisdictions that are responsible for eroding the corporate tax bases of Germany or Ghana.

National commitments have not always been easy to defend in the face of sustained lobbying, despite the general increase in civil society and broader public engagement. International agreement and implementation, meanwhile, has been deeply problematic. Current institutions such as the Organisation for Economic Co-operation and Development (OECD) have proven deficient – both ineffective and biased in favour of certain interests. The OECD's lack of transparency over decision-making, its susceptibility to lobbying and its refusal to provide non-member countries with an equal voice have each contributed to a loss of ambition in its work and the widening, rather than narrowing, of global inequalities in taxing rights between countries.

Tax abuse has continued to grow over the period, especially that of multinational companies, as a result of these failures. Understanding the reasons for this provides greater clarity about the type of institutional changes that are likely to be necessary to change the options for national policymakers and their populations. Identifying what should be done to achieve tax justice therefore entails a combination of national and international measures, and the institutional overhaul necessary to facilitate this effectively and inclusively.

Finally, in the 'Conclusion' of this short book, I suggest the direction of travel for tax justice nationally and globally over the coming decade – the policies and institutional shifts that we may expect, or at least hope, to see, if the movement towards tax justice movement is to continue to change the world we live in. A growing part of any such agenda must address the increasingly extreme threats to planetary sustainability and biodiversity we now face.

background

The two headline features of tax systems are the volume of revenues (normally thought of as a share of the economy, measured by gross domestic product, GDP); and their structure, in particular the balance between direct and indirect taxes.

Tax revenues are typically around 35% to 40% of GDP for high-income countries, including the members of the OECD. The UK has tended to be on the lower side of this, though has seen a rising trend in recent years. For the 2022–23 financial year, UK taxes stood at 36.4% of GDP (according to the Office for Budget Responsibility).

For upper-middle countries (the World Bank's classification for those such as Argentina and Jamaica with per capita national income between $4,466 and $13,845), a tax to GDP ratio of 20% or 25% is not untypical. For lower-middle countries such as Indonesia or Egypt (per capita income between $1,136 and $4,465), a ratio nearer 15% is common. And ratios tend be lower still for low-income countries such as Malawi (12% in 2021) or a country in crisis like Haiti (6%). All data here are from the UNU-WIDER/ICTD Government Revenue Dataset, which was conceived to address the lack of consistent, comparable data on tax revenues across countries and regions of the world (Prichard et al., 2014).

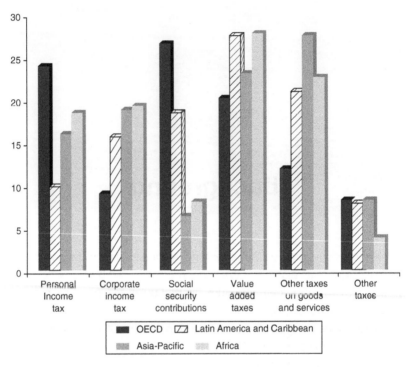

Figure 2.1   Revenue reliance on different types of tax, by region

Source: OECD (2022).

In terms of tax structure (Figure 2.1), OECD countries stand out as more heavily reliant on personal income taxes and social security contributions. Most countries rely heavily on value added taxes (VAT). Countries outside the OECD are more reliant on other taxes on goods and services too, and also are substantially more reliant on corporate income taxes. For OECD countries, direct taxes on incomes and profits, along with social security contributions, account for towards 60% of revenues, while indirect taxes make up the remainder. For most other countries, indirect taxes are responsible for a higher share of revenues, often half.

Above and behind the decisions on size and structure of taxation is of course a state. And as the political scientist Margaret Levi argues in *Of Rule and Revenue*, the 'history of state revenue production is the history of the evolution of the state' (1988, p. 1). In Thomas Hobbes' classic work of political theory, *Leviathan,* the state role is played by a potentially cruel sovereign; and for Levi, the state is by definition predatory. Levi's theory of predatory rule sees the state seeking to maximise revenue (for good or bad use), but bound by constraints in their bargaining power (how much extraction can they enforce); in transactions costs (how wasteful is the raising of revenues); and future discount rates (how concerned are they about future instability).

The Scottish economist Adam Smith had set out in his *Wealth of Nations* (1776, Book V, Chapter 2, Part 2) four canons that he felt should govern taxation. These are proportionality (that taxpayers should contribute according to their ability, that is to say 'in proportion to the revenue which they respectively enjoy under the protection of the state'); certainty and convenience (that the timing, manner and amount of payment should be clearly known, and as convenient as possible for the taxpayer); and efficiency (that the tax should not encourage economically damaging responses).

Jumping forward to the present day and we find that the Scottish government, which operates a range of taxes under devolution from the UK government in Westminster, has adopted Smith's principles and added two further of their own in their *Framework for Tax* (Scottish Government, 2021). The *Framework* warrants some attention in part because it is a substantive, current view of the state's role to tax in a high-income jurisdiction; and in part because there is no obviously equivalent material available for the UK itself.

The UK government's (2020) '10-year Tax Administration Strategy: Building a trusted, modern tax administration system' sounds promising, but on inspection is focused primarily on better use of data, and does not detain itself long on high-level principles: 'The UK has one of the best tax authorities in the world, but HMRC [His Majesty's Revenue and Customs] cannot be complacent. HMRC is already making good progress in introducing a new, digital VAT service through the Making Tax Digital programme, while supporting as many businesses as possible to benefit from the productivity gains of using digital accounting systems. The government wants to go further by extending modern services to more taxpayers and agents.'

The first of the Scottish government's additional principles is 'engage-ment', which reflects a recognition of the social contracting role of tax: 'People and businesses should be able to understand the tax system and governments and tax authorities play a critical role in relation to that. Governments must therefore be open and transparent about tax policies and their decision-making, consulting as widely as possible. This is cru-cial for accountability and trust' (Scottish Government, 2021, p. 3).

The second relates to Smith's efficiency principle, but reflects more clearly the potential for abusive responses to tax. 'Effectiveness: Design of the tax system should focus on ensuring taxes raise the expected revenues and achieve their intended aims. This includes designing taxes that mini-mise opportunities for tax avoidance. The vast majority of taxpayers want to pay the correct amount of tax, and do, but where taxpayers do engage in avoidance practices governments and tax authorities should respond quickly and proactively to tackle them' (Scottish Government, 2021, p. 3).

The Framework for Tax is summarised in Figure 2.2. The intention is that the principles provide the basis for policy choices that ensure the key functions of taxation are delivered, in aid of the Scottish government's strategic objectives. The functions identified are broadly in line with three of the 4 Rs of tax explored in the first chapter: that is, *revenues* to fund public services, *redistribution* to curb inequalities, and *repricing* to change behaviour and stimulate the economy.

The 4th R, the role of tax in building representation, is less evident in the specific functions. It is, however, reflected in the first line of the Framework's vision statement: 'Taxes form part of the fabric of society and we should all be proud of the contribution they make. They are a key component of the social contract' (p. 4).

The dominant international thinking on tax in the last five or six dec-ades has tended to under-emphasise this 4th R. The British economist John Williamson coined the term the 'Washington Consensus' at the end of the 1980s, to describe what he saw in the US and international financial institutions like the International Monetary Fund (IMF) as the set of poli-cies, 'about whose proper deployment Washington [or rather, its political and technocratic elites] can muster a reasonable degree of consensus'.

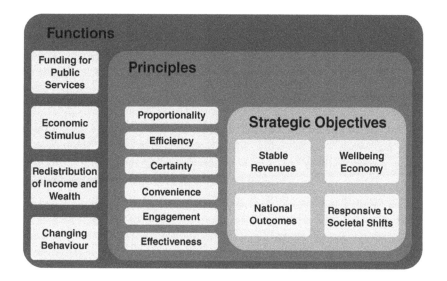

Figure 2.2 The Scottish government's Framework for Tax

Source: Scottish Government (2021), Figure 4.

The Washington Consensus became well known and was also despised by many. It was understood by some as a summary of prevailing policy views in certain circles, as Williamson intended. But for many, it was equally a statement of the mindset that was present in influential high-income countries, *and imposed on many lower-income countries* in the decades before and after his writing. This applies equally to the third of the ten elements in Williamson's framework, which is what has been called more specifically the 'tax consensus'.

Development economists would later summarise the tax consensus as having three main components (Adam & Bevan, 2004; Heady, 2004). First, *neutrality* of the tax system, like Smith's 'efficiency', emphasised the need not to affect incentives. That in practice led to recommendations to pursue liberalisation (removal) of trade taxes, and to introduce sales taxes like VAT in preference to direct taxes in incomes, profits or capital.

Relatedly, the second component recommended pursuing redistributive goals (if governments had any) via expenditure not taxation, on the grounds that this would be less distorting economically. Finally, lower-income countries were encouraged to aim for revenues of the order of 15–20% of GDP (despite those in high-income OECD countries being typically twice that).

The 'tax consensus' reflects the extent to which leading OECD countries, notable among them the UK, had sought to lower their own overall taxes, and to shift the structure away from direct taxes through introduction of VAT-type taxes. The period in question is marked by the longest steady fall in the UK's tax/GDP ratio, from a peak of 36.7% in 1982, to a low of under 30% in 1995–1997 – a period that coincides closely with the Conservative governments of Margaret Thatcher (1979–1990) and her successor John Major (until 1997). Since then, the range has been more constrained, between a low of 30.9% in 2009 and a high of 33.5% in 2021's partial rebound from the first year of the COVID-19 pandemic.

For the UK, and many others including the US (see, e.g., Piketty, 2014), this tax stance pre-1997 was associated with weaker redistribution through tax, and sharply rising inequalities. As the basis for advice to lower-income countries, it stood to promote the same outcomes. More damagingly, it ignored the 4th R of tax: the role of tax in fostering political representation and the social contract (Cobham, 2007).

In the short and even medium term, for high-income countries like the UK, levels of trust, tax morale and the strength of institutions of government could perhaps be taken for granted. Whether that was sustainable is another question. For lower-income countries that already lacked revenue to support an effective state, and with a more recent history of illegitimate (imperial) government, neither trust nor the quality of institutions could be assumed.

Consider a population for whom the recent experience of paying tax has been to a colonial administration that imposed its demands by force, felt little or no accountability to demonstrate useful or inclusive public expenditure, and divided its revenue between the costs of maintaining power and what it could send back to the imperial capital. How quickly can the legitimacy of tax, and the strength of the social contract, be established after independence? Or in southern Europe, when dictators lost power in the later decades of the 20th century in Spain, Portugal and Greece: how soon would levels of tax morale grow? What of eastern Europe, as the Berlin Wall fell and states with them?

It is arguable that in all of these cases, building tax morale and the social contract and supporting the emergence of accountable, democratic governance might – and perhaps should – have been the central priorities for tax policy. But the 'tax consensus' pushed, instead, for the adoption of tax policies that were least likely to bolster tax compliance, according to the evidence surveyed in the first chapter. By stymying redistribution and failing to pursue revenues with which to build a more effective state, and by turning away from direct taxes that are more likely to strengthen the social contract, the dogmatic promotion of the tax consensus looks like a damaging error.

In the UK, meanwhile, the Thatcher–Major years ended with a landslide political swing to the Labour Party and the Blair–Brown government, set (rhetorically at least) on tackling inequality and child poverty, and rebuilding the quality of public services. The 1997 election saw Labour leading with pledges to 'save' the National Health Service and to reduce class sizes for 5, 6 and 7-year-olds – but also *not* to increase income taxes, due to a fear of being labelled as a 'tax and spend' party.

As the evidence in the previous section makes clear, when we weaken our tax systems, for short-term political gains or out of ideological rigidity, we do long-term damage to our own societies. But political incentives do not align well with social aims, and tax policies are all too often influenced by the former rather than the latter. How can the incentives for policymakers become better aligned with the long-term interests of our societies? The movement for tax justice has its roots in that disconnect, and in a desire to defend and strengthen the 'web of generalised reciprocity' that constitutes the social contract. The following chapter explores those roots, and the concept of tax justice.

what do we know about tax justice?

This chapter is divided into three parts. The first surveys the main perspectives on the concept of tax justice. This reveals a broadening and internationalisation of understanding over the last century. It also shows a growing emphasis on international inequalities in taxing rights, both current and historic (but unaddressed).

The second part surveys quantitative and other research on the scale and nature of the problem of tax *in*justice today. In the profit shifting practices of multinational corporations, just as in the 'offshore' tax abuse of wealthy individuals, we'll see a common feature is reliance on financial opacity to avoid scrutiny or detection.

In keeping with the evolution of perspectives on tax justice, a consistent feature of research over recent decades has been to shift understanding away from a flawed and narrow view of 'tax havens' as a discrete group of (typically small island) jurisdictions as responsible for the damage done to most others. The leading role of some major economies like the UK is now recognised. Less widely understood is that 'tax havenry' does not make a jurisdiction's own people immune from tax injustice. On the contrary, most members of these populations can suffer intensely from the policy path chosen.

A brief third section provides an assessment of the damage caused by cross-border tax abuse and sets this in a historical overview going back to the period of formal empire. Understanding the emergence of tax havens, and the power dynamics behind their rise, provides important insights into the patterns and drivers of tax abuse today – and the resistance to reform. It also reveals a pattern of historic and continuing extraction from (former) colonies, which plays a significant role in shaping the world economy today. That informs an argument for a 5th R of tax: namely, that tax should now play a *reparative* role.

Perspectives on tax justice

Tax justice is like an elephant because you recognise it when you see it but it's hard to define.

Tax Justice Network, 2005a

'Tax justice' can mean different things to different people. Its usage and the commonly understood meaning have varied over time. Three main perspectives can be identified in the last century. While they do not directly contradict each other, as each builds upon and extends the previous understanding, the three perspectives are nonetheless quite distinct. The first is primarily domestic, and addresses differences in the tax rates faced by different types of income and people. The second perspective introduces the critical role of 'tax havens' in promoting cross-border abuses of tax and financial regulation, and driving a race to the bottom in tax rates. The third perspective is the most fully global and recognises more prominently the inequalities in taxing rights between different countries, and the international structures that are responsible.

Tax justice I: Domestic focus, equal tax rates

The first and narrowest concept of tax justice is associated with the term's earliest sustained use in the English language. This occurs during a period from the late 1930s, where we find the US Under Secretary to the Treasury speaking to Congress of 'tax justice and progressive taxation' (US Congress, 1939). The term features heavily in debate over taxing financial securities. Tax justice here relates to whether income of different types should be taxed to a common extent, and specifically whether it is fair that income from financial securities should be taxed preferentially less. By the late 1960s, the term had such salience in US politics that it features frequently in Congressional debates and hearings, and in the reports of many trade union bodies.[1] A National Committee for Tax Justice was formed of eminent persons, with a five-point plan including elimination of preferential treatment for capital gains (US Congress, 1969).

This perspective on tax justice is almost exclusively concerned with domestic policy questions, although it has powerful international implications. Its most common expression has been in relation to differentials in tax rates between labour and capital. That is to say, the key question is whether those who make their income from owning capital should be allowed to continue paying lower taxes than those who make their income by their own labour.

In the UK, for example, you pay tax at a rate of 40% on any part of your annual salary above £50,000 (and 45% on anything over £125,000). But if you have income from gains on owning capital, the most you'll pay is just 20%. Meanwhile in the United States, well-funded opponents of (any) capital gains taxation are increasingly aggressive in their pursuit of judicial rulings that such taxes are unconstitutional (see, e.g., Washington State Budget & Policy Center, 2022).

A combination of the more concentrated political influence of capital, and the greater scope for reengineering of capital income, means that the relatively lower taxation of capital income is a common phenomenon across geographies and over time. Figure 3.1 shows the pattern over the last half

---

1 See, e.g., search results for 'tax justice' during 1968–1970, at www.google.com/sear ch?q=%22tax+justice%22&lr=lang_en&tbs=lr:lang_1en,cdr:1,cd_min:1/1/1968,cd_ma x:1/1/1971&tbm=bks&ei=YNYiY7jHNeylur4P6Yaa4A4&start=0&sa=N&ved=2ahUKE wi4956dpZb6AhVshM4BHWmDRuw4KBDy0wNODAyBEEQ&biw=1536&bih=726&d pr=1.25 (accessed 15/9/2022).

a century. Since the 1960s, the average effective global tax rate on income from labour has increased from around 15% to around 25% – that's a rise of around two-thirds. Tax on corporate profits has shown almost the exact opposite trajectory, falling from 25% to well under 20%. Tax on income from capital overall has fallen from above 30% to nearer 25%.

That apparent convergence between the effective tax rates on labour and capital might be interpreted as evidence of success for the first tax justice perspective, but this would be wrong. Bear in mind that the concentration of capital ownership is far, far higher than that of labour – since we can each only do a certain amount of work, and the annual salaries for most of us are within a relatively narrow band. Progressive tax systems should ensure that those on lower salaries are taxed at a much lower rate than those on higher salaries, or indeed than the recipients of typically much higher incomes from capital.

We should therefore expect the average effective tax rate on labour to be much lower, if income from each source is taxed on the same, progressive basis. The fact that the rates have converged indicates that the preferential treatment given to capital has been significantly exacerbated. And the fact that corporate incomes in particular have been taxed on average less than income from labour since the mid-1970s – and that this gap has continued to widen over the following decades – is a further, powerful illustration of the shifts in relative lobbying power worldwide.

While the evidence may suggest a fight that has been lost globally, the issue retains great political salience at the national level. Recent attention in the UK was piqued by prime minister Rishi Sunak's published tax return. Sunak declared roughly £1.6 million of investment income. His effective tax rate was 22%: roughly what a nurse in the National Health Service could expect to pay on their salary (Tax Justice UK, 2023). The difference is due to the much lower tax rate on investment income than on work. That Sunak himself presided over those tax rates, as Chancellor (that is, finance minister) in the period in question, drew further attention to the discrepancy.

Underlying the powerful anger that this perspective on tax justice can generate is the point that different tax treatment of different income types,

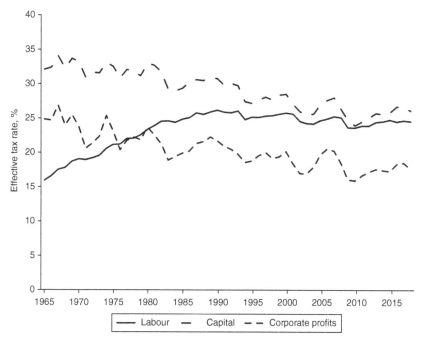

Figure 3.1 Global tax rates on labour, capital and corporate profits

Source: Data from Bachas et al. (2023).

implies unfair treatment of different types of people. In supporting an amicus brief to defend the constitutionality of capital gains tax, Kamau Chege, Executive Director of the Washington Community Alliance, gave this statement: 'As a statewide coalition of dozens of organizations across the state, led by and working in communities of color, the Washington Community Alliance seeks to have an economy that works for all of us. The capital gains tax would rightly take a step to flip Washington's upside-down tax code, in which those with the least are asked to pay the most.'

In countries all around the world, more economically marginalised groups typically receive lower incomes, and rely more on labour income than any other type. This will disproportionately include marginalised racial and ethnolinguistic groups, women-headed households, households including people with disabilities and LGBT+ people (Cobham, 2019). Those facing overlapping inequalities are likely to face a double marginalisation or more. When tax systems are less progressive in general, and discriminate in favour of capital income over labour income, the result will be to drive these inequalities systematically higher.

Professor Dorothy Brown's *The Whiteness of Wealth: How the Tax System Impoverishes Black Americans and How We Can Fix It* (2021) catalogues the racially discriminatory nature of the US tax system, revealing major, structural inequalities of just this type. Analysis of new data also confirms racial bias in the practical application of taxes. Black taxpayers are found to be between 2.9 and 4.7 times more likely to be audited – even though modelling shows that 'maximizing the detection of underreported taxes would *not* lead to Black taxpayers being audited at higher rates' (Elzayn et al., 2023, p. 1, emphasis added). This perspective on tax justice remains a crucial agenda for those concerned with social justice.

Tax justice II: Challenging cross-border tax abuse – and neoliberalism

The second main perspective on tax justice is not inconsistent, but is markedly broader in the policy tools it considers, and more international in its analysis. It should be understood, at least partly, within the context of the rise of 'neoliberal' dogma in the second half of the 20th century. Although sometimes being used as a somewhat contentless pejorative term, 'neoliberal' has a clear meaning. As Slobodian (2020) details, the neoliberal thinkers who emerged from Austria, first, in the 1920s and 1930s, did not seek to undermine the state in general, so much as they sought to harness states and international institutions collectively in order to tie the hands of individual states – in the broader aim of protecting markets from the turbulence of politics and conflict. This included, often explicitly, the desire to strip states of the power to respond to calls for greater social justice, including through significant tax, trade and labour market interventions.

Backed by an opaquely funded, international network of 'think tanks', this movement arguably reached its rhetorical height in the UK and US governments of Margaret Thatcher and Ronald Reagan in the 1980s and 1990s (Maclean, 2017). Significant influence has remained since, within many countries and international institutions also.

Tax justice here can be seen as a response to this once and continuing threat of a deregulatory, 'small state' ideology, which *inter alia* takes high inequality as an acceptable, inevitable element of the trade-off for growth in GDP. In this context, it becomes critically important to make the positive case for tax and financial regulation, along with the state's role to curb inequality. Untying the hands of states by unpicking international, institutional obstacles (and preventing the creation of new ones) was to be combined with re-establishing the legitimacy of states acting nationally to promote social justice.

The importance of this perspective in the Tax Justice Network's first phase perhaps reflects the relatively UK-centric and global North nature of the organisation's founding in 2002/3 (see Christensen, 2012). But the ideological shift to which it responds was and is pervasive, and global in nature. That fact supported the relevance of the perspective as the movement grew internationally.

Here, tax is understood in terms of its overall role in a society. The question of justice relates to the extent to which the tax system can deliver on that potential, for the benefit of all – or is captured to serve narrower interests instead. A major focus is on the threat posed by financial deregulation, and the resulting opportunities both for cross-border tax abuse and for an acceleration of the race to the bottom.

The 'race to the bottom' is based on the idea that countries can 'compete' for international investment by reducing their rates of tax, or the strength of their market regulations, or the protections they provide for workers. The whole notion is inherently flawed because countries cannot compete in the way that an infinite number of companies are supposed to, in the simple economic model of 'perfect competition'.

For one thing, the model relies on a multitude of companies going bust, with effectively no social cost. Countries cannot go bust in the same way, and the human and social costs of economic collapse are huge. And there are only a certain number of countries in the world, only a certain number of places that a business can employ people, use infrastructure, benefit from the rule of law and access to markets, and so on. (As Slobodian, 2023, highlights, this is why the most extreme opponents of effective states have long sought to create new jurisdictions – from freeports to charter cities – and to exploit differences in subnational jurisdictions, from US states and Swiss cantons to UK-dependent territories and apartheid South Africa's 'bantustans'.)

In addition, not all investment is the same. If you aggressively pursue the most mobile capital, the investors who are most easily swayed by a further, marginal reduction in tax or regulation, do you think they will stay for the long term and become productive participants in your economy and society? Or are you effectively choosing a type of investor who will never put down roots, never contribute more than they absolutely have to and be off at the drop of a hat when something even closer to the bottom turns up?

The role of corporate tax havens and 'financial secrecy jurisdictions' comes sharply into view. These terms relate to the countries and dependent territories that are most extreme in blocking transparency and in cutting tax and regulation in order to facilitate abuse elsewhere. This adds further pressure on the countries losing out, to 'compete' harder. Undercut the others, and you will reap the benefits instead, sing the siren voices of the race to the bottom – but of course, there is no bottom. If you go low, someone else will go lower still. How do you compete with jurisdictions that offer a zero per cent tax rate? Tax incentives. Subsidies. Holidays from labour regulation... But at the end, all possible benefit to a country has been 'competed' away, captured by mobile capital.

While the focus on justice remains domestic in this perspective, the threats to that domestic agenda are now clearly understood as international in nature. This broadening of view was accompanied by the understanding that the same issues are prevalent in countries in all regions and at all levels of per capita income – and so tax became a major issue in international development circles.

A resonant case study reflecting the arguments for the equal treatment of income in this context came from ActionAid's 2010 report into the global alcohol multinational, SABMiller. In addition to exposing the company's Ghanaian producer as having paid tax in only one year out of four, it contrasted the multi-million-pound operation with a small beer and food stand operating in the shadow of the brewery. The owner, Marta Luttgrodt, reflected on the multiple taxes that her business was regularly required to prove it had paid – more than SABMiller's operation in most years. 'I don't believe it... if *we* don't pay, they come with a padlock' (ActionAid, 2012, p. 7, emphasis added).

Tax justice III: A global and reparative demand

The first regional network was launched in Nairobi in 2007, Tax Justice Network-Africa. In 2013, the Global Alliance for Tax Justice emerged as the umbrella body for mass campaigning organisations, with a membership made up of regional networks spanning the world: Tax Justice Network-Africa, Red de Justicia Fiscal de América Latina y el Caribe, Tax and Fiscal Justice Asia and Tax Justice-Europe. Each regional network comprises national civil society organisations. These include organisations pursuing broad economic justice aims, and specifically tax justice organisations – ranging from Tax Justice Norge (Norway), to Instituto Justiça Fiscal (Brazil) to Tax Justice Network-Australia.

Today, Tax Justice Network-Africa 'promotes socially just, accountable and progressive taxation systems in Africa [and] advocates for tax policies with pro-poor outcomes and tax systems that curb public resource leakages and enhance domestic resource mobilisation'.[2] The Global Alliance for Tax Justice works 'for a world where progressive and redistributive tax policies counteract inequalities within and between

---

2 https://taxjusticeafrica.net/ (accessed 15/9/2022).

countries, and generate the public funding needed to ensure essential services and human rights.'[3]

This globalisation of the movement gave rise to the third main perspective on tax justice, characterised by a more fully global understanding of the issues and a deeper historical and power analysis.

Cross-border tax abuse is now understood within a centuries-long evolution of illicit financial flows, as the last part of this chapter explores. European empires and settler states have been key actors in the extraction of wealth from lower-income countries – from South Africa to Indonesia, and from India to Argentina. The relative wealth of the first group and the lower per capita incomes of the second are a direct result of those processes of extraction and the power relations that result and persist. Less well understood perhaps is that the period following the end of formal empire has seen an evolution of international rules and practices which has continued that pattern of extraction through tax abuse and other illicit flows.

The same power relations that stem from empire underlie the international rules and norms on tax and financial regulation. Tax justice in this view therefore requires changing global governance arrangements – in particular, as set out in the following chapter, to move rule-making from the exclusive control of the rich countries' club, the OECD, and into a globally inclusive setting at the United Nations. This follows from a belief that institutions unduly dominated by a group of rich countries are unlikely to deliver results that address the tax-related inequalities that exist *between* as well as within countries. In the title of Audre Lorde's famous (1984) essay, 'The Master's Tools Will Never Dismantle the Master's House'.[4]

This perspective offers campaigners a greater opportunity to emphasise solidarity. Rather than seeing some countries as victims of tax abuse and others as havens that benefit from facilitating that abuse, this perspective

---

3 https://globaltaxjustice.org/about-gatj/ (accessed 15/9/2022).

4 '*For the master's tools will never dismantle the master's house.* They may allow us temporarily to beat him at his own game, but they will never enable us to bring about genuine change. And this fact is only threatening to those women who still define the master's house as their only source of support.'

provides a reframing in which most (or even all) people, in most or even all countries, would stand to benefit from unravelling the overall structures that support tax abuse.

Tax can be a social superpower for us all. Understanding our failure to exercise this power is the story of tax justice, and of this chapter.

The scale of tax injustice

I have talked to somebody who works in PwC, and what they say is that you will approve a tax product if there is a 25% chance—a one-in-four chance—of it being upheld. That means that you are offering schemes to your clients—knowingly marketing these schemes—where you have judged there is a 75% risk of it then being deemed unlawful. That is a shocking finding for me to be told by one of your tax officials. I bet it is mirrored by all four accountancy firms sitting here, and I would like you to tell the Committee how you justify that approach.

First of all, I don't know where that came from; I don't recognise that statement. [...]

Do you offer complex structures involving setting up companies in low-tax jurisdictions, such as, in this case, Luxembourg and Jersey [interruption] And Delaware. And the Cayman Islands. This one is Delaware, Jersey and Luxembourg. Do you do that for the purpose of minimising tax?

It will be one of the things taken into account.

UK parliamentary evidence session with PwC head of tax, 2013[5]

---

5 Exchange between then-chair of the Public Accounts Committee, Margaret Hodge MP, and then-head of tax at PwC, Kevin Nicholson. Questions 36, 47 and 48 of evidence session of 31 January 2013 (House of Commons Committee of Public Accounts, 2013).

Definitional questions: Tax abuse, avoidance and evasion

Financially at least, the biggest abuses by far occur among the largest taxpayers (that is, the most profitable multinational companies and the wealthiest individuals) – and those who enable multiple such taxpayers (primarily, the group of accounting firms and law firms that specialise in this area). The leading estimates explored below distinguish between offshore tax *evasion*, largely by individuals hiding assets and income streams; and the tax *abuse* of multinational companies. 'Tax abuse' is used here as a catch-all term for both evasion and avoidance.

Purely domestic cases of tax abuse can be substantial. HMRC (2023) estimates that small businesses alone – which operate almost exclusively domestically – are responsible for tax losses of £20 billion in the last financial year. International cases of abuse in relation to indirect taxes can also be substantial. These include many fraud cases within the EU around customs and VAT. In 2023, for example, the UK completed a £2.3 billion payment to the EU to settle a case in which the UK had been found to have acted as a 'significant hub' for fraud, allowing organised crime groups to import undervalued goods into the EU. The UK had then failed to pass on import duties and VAT payments (BBC, 2023).

Systematic tax abuse, however, is dominated by the cross-border abuse of direct taxes. Direct taxes are levied by states on income and assets, including corporate profits and capital gains. Direct taxes may be defeated by the claim that the income or asset is not taxable. Such a claim takes two main forms. The taxpayer can simply deny their ownership. Or, the taxpayer can deny that the income or asset is taxable by the state in question.

The (false) denial of ownership tends to fall into the category of tax *evasion*. For example: 'I've never seen those banknotes before', 'I have no Swiss bank account', 'I do not own that Jersey company' and so on. The concealment of income or assets in this way is typically assessed as fraudulent, and may well lead to criminal penalties when uncovered.

Tax *avoidance* is an intentionally less clearcut area, and often revolves around whether particular income is taxable by a particular state. In general, avoidance is used in reference to the tax behaviour of multinational companies; while evasion is more typically applied to individuals.

The catch-all term of 'tax abuse' is especially helpful in relation to multinationals. Tax lawyers like to insist on a categorical distinction between avoidance and evasion here, but in practice this obscures more than it reveals, both for public understanding and for the pursuit of rigorous research.

A widely held view is that avoidance is legal by definition. For example, in her 2003 inaugural lecture as KPMG Professor of Taxation Law at Oxford University, Judith Freedman uses the term to cover 'all arrangements to reduce, eliminate or defer tax liability that are not illegal' (Freedman, 2004). Or as a 2012 review for the UK government noted, 'Practically every media report on avoidance now starts with the statement that the activities it is discussing are legal' (Devereux et al., 2012). Both pieces consider how to make anti-avoidance approaches more effective, from this starting point.

In this view, taxpayers arrange their affairs so as to reduce the tax payable. Without fraudulent concealment, they present this arrangement to the tax authorities. If the authorities accept it, the avoidance is considered successful. If the authorities challenge the arrangement and prevail, the avoidance is regarded as unsuccessful. Crucially for the lawyers involved and their clients, even unsuccessful tax avoidance is – in this view – legal.

When lawyers for a tax authority win their court case against a particular tax avoidance scheme, the scheme is deemed to be unlawful. The practitioners would argue that there was uncertainty up until the moment of the court decision. They were therefore acting legally to promote or use the scheme until then, and at that point they would cease immediately.

The UK parliamentary evidence session quoted above highlights a specific issue. This is that the basis for thinking the scheme reasonable in the first place must be considered. In the session, the claim is made that the 'big four' accounting firm PwC was then operating with a willingness to promote schemes that they themselves judged to have only a 25% chance of withstanding challenge. A more common claim is of a 50%

threshold – so that schemes would be promoted if they had the same chance of success as calling heads or tails on the toss of a coin.

But why could it make sense for PwC or others to act in this way? For one thing, if tax cases take a sufficiently long time to come to court, and can then be appealed through various further stages, there may be a significant benefit to the taxpayer over many years. Even if some rate of interest is eventually charged on the outstanding liabilities, the interim period has effectively seen the taxpayer benefit from a loan made out of the public purse.

More importantly, and of greater concern, the willingness to promote very high-risk schemes is likely to reflect a rational calculation of the likelihood of challenge. You might recommend a series of scheme that you judge to have only a very low chance of withstanding a challenge, if you also thought that there was only a very low chance of them being challenged. You might lose most or even all of the challenges that you face, but still enable a great deal of non-payment of tax because of all the schemes that go entirely unchallenged. Quentin (2017) models how tax avoidance schemes introduce a tax risk factor, that under most circumstances will apply an expected transfer of public resources to the taxpayer. Quentin (2019) highlights how, despite some recent improvements, corporate statements of tax risk attitudes are not typically framed as to be consistent with less abusive approaches.

The further complication to the 'avoidance legal/evasion illegal' dichotomy is that it need not map precisely onto the distinction between the tax behaviour of multinational companies, on the one hand, and individual taxpayers on the other. That is, multinational companies and their professional advisers may focus on avoidance but are not incapable of criminal evasion.

To give just one example here: in 2019, the US multinational Google paid around 1 billion euros to settle a case with the French tax authority; 500 million euros of that constituted a penalty for tax *fraud* (NBC, 2019). The tax decision hinged, as is often the case with multinationals, on the location of the real economic activity giving rise to taxable profits. Here,

Google had maintained that employees in Ireland were ultimately responsible for large volumes of sales in France. The tax authority, and ultimately the courts, disagreed.

In 2005, the big four accounting firm KPMG – yes, the proud sponsors of a professorial chair in tax law at Oxford University – 'admitted that it engaged in a fraud that generated at least $11 billion dollars in phony tax losses which, according to court papers, cost the United States at least $2.5 billion dollars in evaded taxes' (Internal Revenue Service, 2005). This was then the largest criminal tax case ever filed, and also saw nine people including six KPMG partners and its former deputy chair face criminal prosecution. It related to the design, marketing and implementation of fraudulent tax shelters.

The clients for KPMG tax shelters were mainly individuals and businesses smaller than the largest multinationals. The case highlights, however, that it would be artificial to draw a hard line between offshore evasion and corporate tax abuse. Offshore evasion may include less sophisticated approaches (the apocryphal small-town dentist with an undeclared offshore bank account, say). But there are large-scale enablers here too, and patterns that more closely resemble the tax behaviours of multinational companies.

Two key features stand out. First, relationships between jurisdictions are important. That covers positive relationships, such as the presence of double tax treaties that can make profit shifting more attractive or feasible. Tax treaties between two countries set certain rates in law. The stated aim is to prevent double taxation of the same income, when a person from one country invests in another. But the resulting limits on the extent to which – for example – Kenya can levy taxes when an investor based in Mauritius repatriates their profits, and that can leave the countries where the real activity takes place with significant revenue losses. By a process of 'treaty shopping', an investor can choose to make an investment into a particular country through the most favourable jurisdiction. That is, the investor can choose which jurisdiction to invest *through* (by setting up a new company in Mauritius, say or the Netherlands), according to which has the best treaty in terms of escaping tax in Kenya, or wherever the investment will be located.

Negative relationships between jurisdictions also matter. Here, the 'shoppers' may be motivated by the absence of arrangements for juridical cooperation or information exchange that can aid the detection of abuse. If the UK dentist wants to be sure that their offshore account will not be revealed to HMRC, for example, then setting up the bank account in the US is probably the best bet – since almost all other financial centres have information exchange agreements with the UK.

Second, and relatedly, cross-border tax abuse thrives on opacity. A lack of transparency is a boon to everyone from individuals seeking to hide offshore income from their home tax authorities, to multinational companies seeking to dodge social condemnation for egregious profit shifting.

The following sections explain the specific characteristics of offshore tax evasion and of multinational tax abuse, and survey the leading estimates of their overall scale and of the international distribution of losses that result.

Offshore tax evasion

This section begins with a brief survey of some of the most high-profile media stories of the last decade, before turning to the research literature on the scale of undeclared offshore wealth and the resulting tax losses.

Leaks and legal cases

As of March 2023, HSBC is Europe's biggest bank. HSBC's strategy announces that 'Our purpose – Opening up a world of opportunity – explains why we exist' (HSBC, 2023). Others have tended to note the bank's incorporation in 1866 as the Hongkong and Shanghai Banking Corporation, and suggest that the British empire's success in the opium wars may do more to explain the original success (e.g. Conne, 2010).

'Opening up opportunity' is a resonant tagline though. As the 'Swiss Leaks' scandal showed, HSBC has indeed opened up opportunities for people around the world.

In 2008, a whistleblowing former employee called Hervé Falciani gave data on HSBC's Swiss private bank to the French government. Later, the data was obtained by *Le Monde* newspaper, and shared with the International Consortium of Investigative Journalists (ICIJ). The data show client accounts from 1988 to 2007. The accounts held funds exceeding US$100 billion, for 106,000 clients from 203 countries and territories in every part of the world. Outside of Switzerland itself, the largest amount of money held was by clients from the UK: almost $22 billion (ICIJ, 2023).

HSBC documentation records numerous staff discussions about the illicit behaviour of clients – and their own role in facilitating this. A 'blood diamond' trader, for whom an account had been opened in Dubai, was noted as 'currently being very careful because he is under pressure from the Belgium tax authorities who are investigating his activities in the field of diamond tax evasion'. An account-holder in Denmark made withdrawals in bundles of kroner since 'it is a criminal act having an account abroad non-declared'. Multiple US account-holders were eventually convicted (Leigh et al., 2015).

HSBC itself was investigated in multiple countries. In general, though, monetary fines were deemed sufficient. The bank has absorbed into its costs of doing business, punishments including a record CHF 40 million fine in Switzerland; €300 million in France; and $192 million in the US (Boland-Rudder, 2015; Hamilton, 2017).

The opportunities that HSBC's Swiss bank opened up were not unique. While the bank defended itself by saying that it had only acquired the Swiss private bank in 1999 and had not yet integrated it into the HSBC ethos, there was further evidence in 2012 of a more systemic issue. The group admitted that its US operations had laundered hundreds of millions of dollars for brutal drug gangs, and faced another record fine of $1.92 billion, as well as five years of monitored probation.

If anyone had expectations that monetary fines would change behaviour, the answer came in 2020. A new set of ICIJ leaks revealed that throughout its probation, 'HSBC continued to provide banking services to alleged crimi-nals, Ponzi schemers, shell companies tied to looted government funds and financial go-betweens for drug traffickers' (Woodman, 2020).

In terms of tax evasion in particular, the Swiss Leaks also form part of a much longer and broader pattern of behaviour. The 'Suisse Secrets' leak of 2022 showed how Credit Suisse, one of the world's biggest private banks, opened and maintained accounts for a quite exceptional range of 'high risk' individuals. In a leak covering 30,000 clients in more than 120 jurisdictions and over CHF 100 billion, investigations revealed a wide range of known criminals, kleptocrats and human rights abusers.

As with HSBC, Credit Suisse has a longer history of involvement in crime. Most obviously, the bank had paid a record $2.6 billion fine to the US in 2014 for conspiring to aid tax evasion. *The Guardian* newspaper's coverage of Suisse Secrets laid out the broader picture: 'Over the past three decades, Credit Suisse has faced at least a dozen penalties and sanctions for offences involving tax evasion, money laundering, the deliberate violation of US sanctions and frauds carried out against its own customers that span multiple decades and jurisdictions. In total, it has racked up more than $4.2 billion in fines or settlements' (Pegg et al., 2022).

Credit Suisse (2022) told the media organisations that it has 'a strict zero tolerance policy towards tax evasion'. But a lawyer for Credit Suisse whistleblowers suggested that it would strain credibility to think all the catalogued behaviour simply represents individual policy violations. 'The bank likes to say it's just rogue bankers. But how many rogue bankers do you need to have before you start having a rogue bank?'[6]

This is a key point. Offshore evasion has not developed at random, with a few people just happening not to tell their home tax authorities about some foreign holdings. Each major leak adds to the evidence of a pattern of behaviour among leading international professionals. In some cases, it seems the enabling of tax evasion is simply not a concern. In others, it appears to be an active aim of operations.

---

6 Jeff Neiman, 'a Florida-based attorney' quoted by Pegg et al. (2022).

A consistent feature of almost every case of proven wrongdoing is the claim that the evidence relates to the past, and such behaviour is no longer allowed. Credit Suisse provides a helpful case study of the plausibility of these statements.

The US Senate Finance Committee published in March 2023 a report covering the previous two years – exactly the period of Credit Suisse's statement of zero tolerance. The committee 'found that Credit Suisse violated key terms of its plea agreement with the Department of Justice'. This included concealing more than $700 million relating to the wealthiest US citizens alone. As such, the committee noted that 'Credit Suisse enabled what appears to be potentially criminal tax evasion to go undetected for almost a decade'.

Perhaps the most famous leak so far is the 2016 Panama Papers, from the law firm Mossack Fonseca. Some 2.6 terabytes of data were leaked to the German newspaper *Süddeutsche Zeitung*, and shared with the ICIJ and its partners. The data cover four decades of operations by one of the world's leading firms in the incorporation of offshore entities, showing that they worked with 'more than 14,000 banks, law firms, company incorporators and other middlemen to set up companies, foundations and trusts for customers' (ICIJ, 2017).

It is not the case, of course, that all of these entities were established for tax evasion or other nefarious purposes. But overwhelmingly, the entities that were established had in common a high level of financial secrecy in relation to the size and ownership of any assets and income streams held.

Among the banks that requested the most offshore entities for their clients, the top five includes Credit Suisse and HSBC (twice – in the shape of the private Swiss bank that formed the basis of the Swiss Leaks, and also the HSBC private bank in Monaco). Alongside UBS (the Swiss bank that recently rescued Credit Suisse), the other leading players are banks and trust companies from Luxembourg, and trust operations from the UK's Crown Dependencies Jersey and Guernsey.

The leaks reveal one part of a broadly professionalised, global system of creating opaque, offshore entities. Bear in mind that Mossack Fonseca was just one company, albeit an important one, among many offering this service over decades. Subsequent, even bigger leaks, such as the Pandora Papers in 2021, showed other angles of the secrecy trade – most notably, the enormous scale of hidden flows through anonymous US trusts, led by South Dakota.

The big numbers: From anecdotes to estimates

There is now a broad empirical literature offering insights into the global scale of the phenomenon, including the tax implications (for a full review, see Cobham & Janský, 2020). The economist Gabriel Zucman (2015) documented how the declared ownership of Swiss bank accounts has shifted, since the 1980s, from named individuals to 'sham corporations'. This reflects the broader trend of growing layers of ownership, in keeping with the gradual development of requirements for transparency and information exchange.

Against this backdrop, quantitative estimates have necessarily been built on imperfect data. Indeed, were the data to be perfect, the problem would be largely eliminated – since tax abuse is only possible without such transparency. Early estimates include a study for the Tax Justice Network (2005b), which put the total of assets held offshore at roughly US$11.5 trillion (with an implied tax revenue loss of $255 billion annually).

Two main approaches to estimating the scale of undeclared offshore wealth now dominate the literature that has developed since 2005. The first approach generates estimates of the scale of illicitly accumulated offshore wealth. These are constructed by estimating, on the basis of anomalies in statistics on international trade and financial positions, the extent of undeclared assets that may have been built up over time outside of owners' home countries.

Major work includes the long-running series of studies by economists Léonce Ndikumana and James Boyce (e.g. 1998, 2003, 2010, 2011a), focused on accumulated African capital held offshore; and work by James Henry (2012) for the Tax Justice Network which takes a global approach, and also triangulates with private bank data and additional sources.

Ndikumana and Boyce (2000; Boyce & Ndikumana, 2011b) are responsible for the finding that the continent of Africa is a net creditor to the world, rather than a net debtor as was once widely assumed. That is, far from the common perception that African countries rely on borrowing and charity from others, this evidence shows that since 1970 (and likely long before that), African countries have in fact been consistent suppliers of capital to the rest of the world – and should be repaid as such.

The analysis to establish this fact combines two main elements. First, anomalies in the declared value of goods crossing borders, after allowing for trade costs, reveal a substantial undeclared value being extracted. Second, a similar approach to capital account anomalies, using national balance of payments data (and adjusting for exchange rate fluctuations, debt write-offs and the likely underreporting of remittances), shows large undeclared sums.

Ndikumana and Boyce use the resulting time series of country-level volumes of unexplained value (out)flows, together with conservative assumptions on cumulative returns, to construct series of the estimated, accumulated illicit capital held undeclared outside each country. That is, they add up the amounts of money leaving African countries each year, allowing for it to be invested with some return, and work out what the total would be worth over time. Their cumulative estimate for this illicit stock over 1970–2015, for a representative sample of 30 African countries, stands at US$1.4 trillion; and $1.8 trillion allowing for interest earnings. As at 2015, the total external debt of the same group of countries stood at just under half a trillion dollars (Ndikumana & Boyce, 2018).

A similar combination of approaches to trade misinvoicing and capital account anomalies applied by the US advocacy group Global Financial Integrity has generated broadly parallel projections for annual flows for a wider set of countries, allowing for different assumptions in some areas.

For estimates of the global stock of illicitly extracted capital, the closest approach is that of James Henry (2012). Henry views the trade data as insufficiently reliable, and instead combines a capital account anomalies approach with triangulation with private bank data on asset holdings; and with an offshore investor portfolio model in which data from the Bank for

International Settlements on cross-border deposits by non-bank investors is scaled up to allow for other, unrecorded asset types. In this way, the work generates a range of estimates which reflect the inevitable uncertainty about just how much is deliberately hidden.

For the global total, the range of undeclared offshore assets estimated by Henry is between $21 trillion and $32 trillion. The Credit Suisse Global Wealth Report for 2011 puts the total of global wealth at $231 trillion, implying that between 9% and 14% of global wealth may be held undeclared offshore.

You might be surprised, incidentally, given the flurry of scandals about its behaviour, to see that Credit Suisse sponsors a product which is useful to estimate the scale of tax abuse. But in truth it is a feature, rather than a bug. Professional enablers of tax abuse often seem to attach their brand names to products that project an air of responsibility and of plausible, academic engagement. The Oxford University Centre for Business Taxation was initially funded by the group of finance directors of the largest UK-listed companies, for example, and the likes of HSBC remain among their donors (OUCBT, 2023).

PwC meanwhile was long proud of its collaboration with the World Bank on Paying Taxes, a deeply ideological ranking of countries that scored them higher simply for having lower and fewer taxes on business. They may be less proud today, perhaps, as the World Bank was forced to shut down the Doing Business rankings of which Paying Taxes was a part, after a scandal over corruption in the assessment that threatened to bring down the entire institution. According to the external investigation ordered by the World Bank, Paying Taxes was one of three indicators manipulated, apparently in order to improve China's ranking (WilmerHale, 2021).

None of this is to cast aspersions on the good intentions of individuals who have carried out research under these conditions. But in terms of companies' commitments to improve the effectiveness of taxation, or to reduce tax abuse, their involvement should be treated with the same scepticism that greets tobacco companies emphasising the health benefits of vaping or the risks of illicit trade if taxes are raised, and fossil fuel companies flexing their green credentials. Tax-washing is a tool of the enablers' game.

The second main approach to estimating undeclared offshore wealth is that of Alstadsæter, Johannesen and Zucman (2018), and the latter's earlier solo work (Zucman, 2013, 2014, 2015). This exploits a different anomaly, found in data on international investment positions. In total, jurisdictions around the world declare a higher value of liabilities in financial securities than they do of assets. To put that another way: people consistently claim that they owe more money (or similar) to others than people confess to own or to being owed. The implication is that people are consistently failing to declare a share of their financial assets, and because the reporting is at the level of jurisdictions, it is possible to identify those responsible for the largest under-declaration. This is argued to reflect the fact that 'tax havens' will report less than fully about the assets of foreigners, and so the gap can be used to estimate the global total of offshore wealth.

As Switzerland, unusually, does report in detail on those assets, it is possible to extrapolate from that data in order to fill the gaps in reporting. This allows the authors to remove, for example, the likely share of cross-border deposits held by corporations and focus only on the assets of households. It also provides the basis to draw out country-level shares of the global total, which support further estimates of national tax losses.

The resulting global estimates of offshore wealth are of the order of 10% of world GDP, and broadly stable over time since 2001. For the benchmark year of 2007, the estimate is $5.6 trillion: somewhat lower than the interview-based estimate of Boston Consulting Group, or that of James Henry (2012).

Through their quite different approaches, Zucman and Henry provide almost identical estimates of the global tax revenue loss: approximately $190 billion.

The most recent update of the Zucman et al. approach has been published by the consultancy ECORYS, for the European Union. Their 2021 study updates the findings to 2018. It shows an increase to offshore wealth holdings of US$9.8 trillion, or 11.4% of global GDP. This is a surprising finding to the extent that a new multilateral instrument for information exchange about foreign bank accounts was fully operational by this stage; we discuss this further in the following chapter.

The ECORYS total, combined with the Zucman et al. approach to generate country-level estimates, forms the basis for the annual study, the State of Tax Justice (Tax Justice Network, 2023). This report provides country-level estimates of the scale of revenue losses suffered by each country. It also goes further and attributes responsibility for others' losses, on the basis of jurisdictions' combined characteristics of financial secrecy and of higher than expected cross-border deposits, supported by regression analysis.

The latest offshore evasion estimate from the State of Tax Justice 2023 is of global tax losses of $169 billion. Three main groups are identified as predominantly responsible. First, the UK 'spider's web'. This is the UK and its dependent territories: the Crown Dependencies such as Jersey, and the British Overseas Territories (BOTs) such as Cayman, many of which are aggressive actors in the provision of the financial secrecy that drives tax evasion. The UK spider's web is estimated to be collectively responsible for more than half of the losses suffered around the world due to offshore tax evasion: $85 billion.

The second group is the 'axis of avoidance'. These are the four jurisdictions identified as primarily responsible for corporate tax abuse (as I explore in the following section). The jurisdictions, in addition to the UK and its web of dependent territories, are the Netherlands, Luxembourg and Switzerland. It turns out that they play a key role for offshore evasion also. Collectively, they are responsible for $111 billion of losses, or 66% of the global total. The third group is the set of rich countries that make up the Organisation for Economic Co-operation and Development (the OECD). They together are responsible for over 90% of the losses suffered, some $156 billion.

Two broad conclusions can be drawn from the research. First, the scale of annual, worldwide revenue losses due to offshore tax evasion is likely in a range above $150 billion. At the country level, those losses are substantial for many (including the UK), both in absolute terms and as a share of total tax revenues. Second, a small group of the richest countries are primarily responsible – and the worst actor by far is the UK and its web of dependent territories.

A complementary method of exploring responsibility is based on a more qualitative assessment of the role each jurisdiction plays in promoting tax evasion. The Financial Secrecy Index is a ranking on that basis, first published by the Tax Justice Network in 2009 (see Cobham et al., 2015).[7] The index is based on two elements, one of which measures the *secrecy* of each jurisdiction and the other of which measures the jurisdiction's *scale* in global finance.

The secrecy score ranges from zero, indicating that the jurisdiction offers no secrecy at all, to 100, indicating the provision of comprehensive financial secrecy. The secrecy score is based on 20 indicators, across four main components (registration of ownership; transparency of legal entities; the integrity of tax administration and financial regulation; and international cooperation). Each indicator in turn is based on assessment of the legal and de facto position of the jurisdiction in question.

The resulting secrecy score is combined with the second element, a global scale weight. This reflects the importance of the jurisdiction in the provision of financial services to non-residents. The scale weight is constructed for each jurisdiction as their share of the global total of financial services exports. For example, the UK accounts for 14% of the global market for financial services provided to non-residents, and the United States 26%, whereas the Bahamas accounts for 0.07% and Liberia 0.04%.

There are two main reasons to combine the two elements: fairness and effectiveness. It would seem unfair to assess a small jurisdiction that provides little or no financial services, as if its secrecy were as damaging as that of a major financial centre like the United States, for example.

---

7 The full index including all editions and latest methodology is available at http://fsi.taxjustice.net.

And equivalently, it does seem fair to recognise that the major players have a greater responsibility (their secrecy can enable much more damage). In terms of effectiveness, there will be little gain for the world if all the least important jurisdictions become more transparent, but the big players are unchanged.

The combination of the two elements therefore ensures that the secrecy of bigger actors is weighted more highly, and that jurisdictions evaluated as highly secretive *but which do not participate meaningfully in global financial services* and therefore do not pose a high risk to others are not elevated to the top of the ranking. Similarly, a jurisdiction of medium secrecy that is a major global player like the UK will be ranked more highly precisely because its secrecy *does* pose a greater risk to others.

The Financial Secrecy Index 2022 displays this logic in action. The US is not the most financially secretive jurisdiction in the world, or even among the top five most secretive jurisdictions. But because it accounts for a full quarter of global financial services exports, the substantial secrecy of the US poses by a distance the greatest risk to others.

Table 3.1 Top five jurisdictions in the Financial Secrecy Index 2022

Ranking	Jurisdiction	Secrecy Score	Global Scale Weight	FSI Value	FSI Share
1	United States	67	25.8%	1951	5.74%
2	Switzerland	70	3.91%	1167	3.43%
3	Singapore	67	5.64%	1167	3.43%
4	Hong Kong	65	3.87%	927	2.73%
5	Luxembourg	55	11.32%	804	2.36%
...					
13	UK	47	14.14%	547	1.61%

The UK sits in 13th, behind the leading Overseas Territory (British Virgin Islands – BVI) in 9th place and Crown Dependency (Guernsey) in 10th.

The UK spider's web has a collective FSI Share of 10.5%, which would put it far clear of the US in first place if assessed as a single entity.

The other 'axis of avoidance' countries (those with greatest responsible for corporate tax abuse) also occupy leading spots here: Switzerland in 2nd, Luxembourg 5th and Netherlands 12th. Adding these gives a combined FSI Share of 17.9%. Combining even just the five other OECD members in the top 20 (US, Japan, Germany, Cyprus, South Korea) adds a further 13%, confirming again the dominant responsibility of OECD countries and their dependent territories.

In an echo of HSBC's tagline, the UK spider's web and indeed much of the OECD's membership seem to be involved in 'opening up opportunity' – for cross-border tax evasion. At the same time, the OECD has often been given a lead role as the institution to carry forward international reforms. That role, and the significant concerns it poses, are explored in the following chapter. Many concerns arise also in relation to the OECD's role on corporate tax – the other major area of cross-border tax abuse.

Multinational tax abuse

Similar to the last, this section surveys some of the most high-profile media stories of the last decade, before turning to the research literature (this time on the scale of corporate profit shifting) and the resulting tax losses.

Public attitudes and media coverage

There is broad consensus among both public and policymakers that companies (of any size) should declare their profits, and pay the tax due, in the place where those profits arise. As polling for the Institute of Business Ethics shows, corporate tax abuse has been the UK public's gravest concern in terms of business ethics in every single survey since the question was introduced in 2013 (IBE, 2022). It is now an absolute priority for almost half of those surveyed – while at most only a quarter of respondents identified any other issue as a priority.

The consensus is built on a more or less continual stream of public demonstrations that companies do *not* pay tax where they make their profits. And yet barely 15 years ago, campaigners were celebrating the first major frontpage news story on the subject. After a painstaking investigation, *The Guardian* newspaper of 6 November 2007 ran the banner headline: 'Revealed: How multinational companies avoid the taxman' (Lawrence & Griffiths, 2007; Tax Justice Network, 2007).

The news story addressed the apparent profit shifting of major banana-producer companies, and the use of Jersey as a tax haven. Associated 'explainer' articles provided readers with a basic understanding of the mechanics of tax avoidance.

For current audiences, this could hardly be news. So accustomed are we now to headlines about the tax behaviour of specific, named multinationals, from Apple to Vodafone, that this would barely register today. Investigative journalism on corporate tax matters reached a new level during the 2010s, above all through the sweeping revelations of the International Consortium of Investigative Journalists.

One of the ICIJ's first major stories was LuxLeaks in 2014. This involved a set of documents leaked by whistleblowers from inside PwC. The documents reveal the big four accounting firm's role in securing secret deals from Luxembourg that saved billions of dollars in tax for multinational clients from FedEx to IKEA. Many of the deals took advantage of 'hybrid loans', so that a given transaction could be presented differently in Luxembourg and another jurisdiction, leading to tax reductions in both.

PwC staff would negotiate the often highly complex deals in secret with Luxembourg tax officials. A ruling obtained for US pharmaceutical company Abbott Laboratories, for example, involved 79 steps including companies in Cyprus and Gibraltar. Despite the complexity, the written proposals of typically 20 to 100 pages which were then submitted to request a tax ruling were often approved by Luxembourg authorities on the very same day.

When the leaks became public, Luxembourg denied most of the claims. The European Commission pledged to investigate, but somehow did not manage to do so during the following five years under the presidency of former Luxembourg prime minister Jean-Claude Juncker.

The EU did start to require that member states declare such rulings with cross-border tax components – but as with Credit Suisse and others, any claims to have reformed were undermined by subsequent revelations.

Seven years later, the LuxLetters revealed a further loophole being heavily exploited. Instead of requesting tax rulings, multinationals or their advisers would write an 'Information Letter' to the Luxembourg tax authority. This would detail the amount of tax the company intends to pay. Then, if there is no response, the letter is considered to be adopted and the companies pay tax accordingly. Should the tax authorities disagree, a meeting takes place in person or by phone, and a resolution is reached. The authorities have never, it seems, challenged an Information Letter in court (Dihmis, 2021). Crucially, for the Luxembourg authorities to be compliant with EU law, they must hold that the Information Letters do not constitute tax rulings, and therefore that they are under no obligation to share them with EU tax authorities.

In response to the reporting of *Le Monde*, *Süddeutsche Zeitung*, *El Mundo*, *Woxx* and IrpiMedia in collaboration with the Tax Justice Network (TJN) and the Signals Network, the Luxembourg authorities issued what appeared to be a comprehensive rebuttal (Luxembourg, 2021): 'The claims made are false and entirely unsubstantiated… In Luxembourg, rulings are strictly regulated and advance rulings issued by the Luxembourg tax administration are issued through an Advance Rulings Commission and are valid for a maximum period of five years. The number of such rulings has decreased significantly and reached 44 in 2020, which corresponds to a decrease of more than –90% between 2015 and 2020.'

The specific denial is less than convincing, however: 'there is no such thing in Luxembourg as an informal or oral confirmation by tax authorities of a taxpayer's tax position based on letters written either by taxpayers themselves or their tax advisors. Any such correspondence with the tax administration *would be purely unilateral*, and can in no way be considered as binding on the tax administration or even be interpreted as confirmation of a given tax situation' (emphasis added).

This, in effect, confirms the claim made by the investigation: that the authorities *do not* provide confirmation in response to the LuxLetters, presumably in order precisely to justify the claim that no ruling *of the sort that would have to be notified to the EU* has been issued.

We see time and again that after being 'caught', or the rules being tightened, the enablers of abuse simply look for a way around. This reflects the central issue in international tax rules today, which is that they have become a game. There is no effective backing for the principle that tax should be paid where activity takes place, largely because of decisions taken a century ago.

The imperial powers at the League of Nations decided in the 1930s that international tax should follow the separate entity accounting approach, resting upon the arm's-length principle (Picciotto, 1992). This requires each subsidiary within a multinational group to be taxed separately, in whichever country it operates. The profit made by each entity must therefore be assessed. That profit will of course depend on the prices that the entity pays, and receives, for the goods and services that it purchases and sells to others.

Since most entities within the group will be transacting with each other, and not only with independent other companies, the problem is how to ensure that the right prices are applied to those intra-group transfers. In theory, this 'transfer pricing' should mirror the prices that independent entities would use to transact with each other – that is, arm's-length prices. But in practice, those prices are often uncertain and increasingly do not exist at all. When multinationals charge their subsidiaries to use their brand or other intellectual property, for example, and such a transaction never occurs in the open market, what is the arm's-length price? The game for multinationals and their tax advisers is how to create transfer prices, or indeed entirely new transactions, such that as much of the group's profit as possible ends up in places where it faces the lowest tax rate possible.

As profit-shifting approaches become more complex and central to business decision-making, some corporate structures are so dominated by entities in 'tax havens' and secrecy jurisdictions that they suggest the business dog has been wagged by the tax tail. Investors, like society, lose out in this scenario. Analysis of the effective tax rates paid by companies listed on the London Stock Exchange shows that shareholders do not receive higher returns when a lower tax rate is engineered – but they do bear greater risks (Brooks et al., 2016).

Big numbers: From anecdotes to estimates

Since the mid-2010s, a combination of greater research focus and improved data availability have shed more light on the national and global implications of the patterns of behaviour revealed. The research literature on corporate tax abuse is broader and deeper than that on offshore evasion, encompassing a wide range of approaches and estimates of the extent and nature of the problem (for a full review, see Cobham & Janský, 2020).

The take-off in abuses of transfer pricing is most clearly demonstrated in a study of the scale of profit shifting by US-headquartered multinationals. The US is one of the only countries in the world that consistently gathered data for decades on the operation of its multinationals in individual countries, and publishes it in aggregate form. That allows a comparative analysis over time of the extent to which US multinationals do or don't pay tax in the places that they do business.

The findings show that in the early 1990s, US multinationals were shifting around 5% of their global profits away from the location of the underlying real activity. Then things took off. By the end of that decade, the share of profits shifted had doubled to around 10%. By the early 2010s, it had reached 25%–30% (Cobham & Janský, 2019).

Recent developments in the research literature include national studies that benefit from improved access to administrative data. For example, the economist (and now research fellow with the Tax Justice Network) Katarzyna Bilicka worked directly with corporate returns in the HMRC Data Lab to produce new and much higher estimates of the scale of tax loss suffered by the UK (Bilicka, 2019). The findings show that subsidiaries of foreign multinationals are much more likely to declare zero profits than similar UK standalone firms. That is, where comparable domestic firms declare profits and pay tax, the subsidiaries of multinationals do neither. As a result, the ratio of taxable profits to assets for subsidiaries is only around half that of UK firms. The implied tax losses are of the order of £25 billion a year. So, either multinationals are systematically very bad at handling their investments in the UK – or the UK is systematically bad at ensuring that appropriate amounts of taxable profits are declared.

In related work, Bilicka (2022) provides a clear answer to a question often raised about UK corporate tax: What explains the apparent puzzle that corporate profits as a share of GDP have risen so strongly, but the tax contribution has not? Bilicka's answer is clear: while domestic firms have paid an increasing share of corporate tax revenues, multinationals have sharply lowered theirs. The scale is striking: by the end of the period studied (2000–2014), over 70% of all assets reported on UK company balance sheets were held by companies that were part of a multinational group *and paid no tax*.

Ludwig Wier and Gabriel Zucman's (2022) work offers the longest-term perspective. The authors build on previous work with Thomas Tørsløv to construct a dataset covering the period from 1975 to 2019. They use data on profit–wage ratios to identify the excess profitability of foreign firms operating in 'tax havens'. Bilateral balance of payments data is then used to allocate the shifted profits back to the original source countries and calculate the forgone tax accordingly.

The findings speak to the cumulative effects of the international failures of tax, and of tax justice. First, corporate profits worldwide have increased at a pace far outstripping the growth of global income. That is, a growing share of global economic activity is now captured in the form of corporate profits. Second, the profits of multinationals in particular – which the authors define as profits booked by corporations outside of their headquarters country – have risen, and much more sharply than have profits overall. Figure 3.2 illustrates these two points.

Wier and Zucman's third main finding is that the impact on lost tax revenue has been punishing. The share of multinational profits (in their definition) shifted to tax havens has risen from under 2% in the 1970s to 37% – which as a share of global profits is a rise from 0.1% to around 7%. Lost revenues have risen from under 0.1% in the 1970s to 10%. Given the growth of profits, corporate tax revenues should have grown by around a third (as a share of global income) since 1975. Instead these revenues have stagnated, with the effective tax rate falling by around a third.

The failure to fix the international tax rules, even as abuse exploded over the course of decades, has left a highly distorted structure in place. As Figure 3.2 shows, there is no evidence of any positive impact from recent changes such as the first BEPS process or the Trump administration's Tax Cuts and Jobs Act: the sharpest rising line on Figure 3.2 is the share of multinationals' profits that are shifted to tax havens.

In terms of understanding the picture at national level, the biggest breakthrough in recent times has been the publication of partially aggregated statistics from the country-by-country reporting of multinationals. This reporting was introduced following sustained campaigning by the tax justice movement, and progress there is discussed in the next chapter. For research purposes, however, the aggregate statistics provide the clearest perspective thus far on patterns of profit shifting by country.

The most detailed analysis thus far is that of Javier Garcia-Bernardo and Petr Janský (2023). They model to extreme non-linearity that characterises the relationship between the cost and the extent of profit shifting. That is, they capture the fact that at low tax rates, even small changes can drive large movements in profit shifting; while for changes at higher tax rates, there is much less effect. Their results are able to cover some 192 countries – far more than studies using any other data source – and are broadly comparable to others.

Garcia-Bernardo and Janský find that profit shifting in 2016 (the first year of aggregate country-by-country reporting statistics) had already reached $1 trillion. A small number of tax havens with very low effective tax rates account for the great bulk of this; namely, Cayman, Luxembourg, Netherlands, Switzerland, Singapore, Bermuda and Puerto Rico.

Figure 3.2   The rise and rise of global profit shifting

Source: Author's elaboration from findings of Wier and Zucman (2022) and Tørsløv et al. (2023).

The related study, drawing on the same data and the insights of these authors, is the corporate tax abuse component of the Tax Justice Network's State of Tax Justice reports. This uses a misalignment model, in keeping with the earlier study of US data. The aim is to compare the actual distribution of profit with an alternative distribution that would apply if profits were fully aligned with the location of multinationals' real economic activity (that is, their sales and employment).

This is in keeping with the single, agreed goal of the G20 group of countries, when they first mandated the OECD to deliver reforms. Specifically, they committed to the goal of reducing this misalignment. As noted earlier in this chapter, public surveys in the UK show strong support for this view also: that companies should pay tax where their real business is done. The State of Tax Justice analysis therefore provides a simple measure of how far, globally, the actual position departs from that goal. At the national level, it identifies the jurisdictions most responsible for the resulting tax losses suffered by others.

The latest corporate tax abuse estimate from the State of Tax Justice is of global tax losses of $311 billion. The UK 'spider's web' is estimated to be collectively responsible for over a quarter of the losses ($84 billion), and the 'axis of avoidance' (the UK web, plus Netherlands, Luxembourg and Switzerland) for over half ($163 billion). The OECD countries (and their dependent territories) together are responsible for 70% of the losses suffered, $219 billion.

Again then, although for even larger losses, a similar pattern emerges to that for offshore tax evasion. Members of the rich countries' club, the OECD, are responsible for the bulk of the revenue losses that they themselves suffer, as well as lower-income countries. Among these, a small number of countries, led by the UK and its web of dependent territories, are the key actors.

As with the Financial Secrecy Index in the case of offshore evasion, a complementary method of exploring responsibility is based on a more qualitative assessment of the role each jurisdiction plays in promoting corporate tax abuse. The Corporate Tax Haven Index (CTHI) is a ranking on that basis, first published by the Tax Justice Network in 2019 (Ates et al., 2021).[8] The index has a parallel structure to the Financial Secrecy Index, with two elements: a 'haven score' and a scale weight.

The haven score ranges from zero, indicating that the jurisdiction offers no scope for corporate tax abuse, to 100, indicating that there is unrestrained scope. The score is based on 20 indicators, across five main components (the lowest available corporate tax rate; the extent of loopholes and gaps; transparency; commitment to tackling corporate tax abuse; and the aggressiveness of tax treaties). Each indicator in turn is

---

8 The full index including all editions and latest methodology is available at https://cthi.taxjustice.net/.

based on assessment of the legal and de facto position of the jurisdiction in question, and focuses on the tax treatment by jurisdictions of local subsidiaries of foreign multinationals.

The 20 indicators are combined into a single haven score. The global scale weight in this case shows the degree of multinationals' activity in each jurisdiction (as a percentage of the global total of multinationals' foreign direct investment). The scale weight and haven score are then combined to ensure that the index treats jurisdictions of different size fairly, and that the ranking effectively identifies those that pose the greatest risk to others.

Table 3.2 Top jurisdictions in the Corporate Tax Haven Index 2021

Ranking	Jurisdiction	Haven Score	Global Scale Weight	CTHI Value	CTHI Share
1	British Virgin Islands	100	2.3%	2853	6.4%
2	Cayman Islands	100	1.9%	2663	6.0%
3	Bermuda	100	1.6%	2508	5.7%
4	Netherlands	80	11%	2454	5.5%
5	Switzerland	89	3.4%	2261	5.1%
...					
13	UK	69	7.3%	1382	3.1%

As Table 3.2 shows, the UK sits again in 13th, but here its dependent territories take the top three spots (and Jersey sits 8th). Assessed as a single entity, the UK spider's web would have a collective CTHI Share of 31.2%, and completely dominate the ranking.

The other 'axis of avoidance' countries make up the top six, with Netherlands and Switzerland followed by Luxembourg (6th). Adding these gives a combined CTHI Share of 46%. Combining the four other OECD members in the top 20 (Ireland, Cyprus, Belgium and France) adds a further 11%. Once again, and even in the area of corporate tax abuse where the OECD has most prominently positioned itself as leading international reforms, it is the organisation's own member countries that are responsible for the majority of revenue losses suffered worldwide. And it is the UK once again that with its web of dependent territories poses the greatest risk to others.

Harms and history

Looking across the assembled research on offshore evasion and corporate tax abuse, three elements emerge consistently. First, the great bulk of responsibility lies with a small group of high-income countries (and their dependent territories). This holds true regardless of whether we consider corprorate or individual offshore tax abuse, and largely regardless of the quantitative or qualitative approach taken, or the data used. It also holds broadly true in the sense that the immediate actors (individual and corporate taxpayers and their professional enablers) are overwhelmingly from those same states, and it is those states that have (most of) the power to set rules to change behaviour.

Second, again by whichever approach is taken, it is clear that the major economies are also the biggest losers to cross-border tax abuse in *absolute* terms. Of the $480 billion of losses identified in the State of Tax Justice 2023 report, countries classified as 'high-income' and 'upper-middle income' by the World Bank suffered $433 billion. On average, the loss is equivalent to around 9% of those countries' annual public health budgets (Tax Justice Network, 2021).

Third, and again it is a common finding across different approaches, it is lower-income countries that suffer the most intense losses. Countries classified by the World Bank as 'low' and 'lower-middle' income bear almost no responsibility but are estimated to suffer $47 billion of tax losses. This smaller absolute value is much more important in the context of their economies and their states. The sum is equivalent to 49% of these countries' public health budgets, making the losses almost five times more intense on this metric than those suffered by higher-income countries.

For countries at all levels of per capita income, the true losses are larger than the direct estimates presented here. Additional indirect losses arise where governments reduce statutory and effective tax rates to counter the direct losses, from the misplaced belief or ideological conviction that this will attract investment. Researchers at the International Monetary Fund estimate that, at a global level, indirect losses from global corporate tax abuse are at least three times larger than direct losses (Crivelli et al., 2016). Other studies suggest a substantially higher range (Cobham & Jansky, 2018 find that indirect effects may be 4–6 times larger than the direct effects; Garcia-Bernardo et al., 2021 find a wider range of 2–15 times).

Wier and Zucman's (2022) study confirms that, all else being equal, corporate tax revenues would have been around a third larger in relation to global income – had the losses due to tax abuse not brought about this sustained downward pressure on effective tax rates. Such a scale of loss has implications well beyond revenue.

Recall the 4 Rs of tax: revenue, redistribution, repricing and political representation. The set of jurisdictions that drive cross-border tax abuse, and set the international rules and institutions that do not prevent it, are culpable not just for financial losses but for the denial of effective statehood – and better prospects for improved human experiences – to billions of people.

Those same effects play out in higher-income countries like the UK, with tax systems that are less able to address overlapping inequalities and governments that are less likely to respond to public preferences for such action. The most intense effects will be in lower-income countries though, which bear little or no responsibility for the issue.

Redressing the global inequalities in taxing rights, and the far-reaching human and social costs they impose, is therefore the central challenge of tax injustice. The argument can be extended, too, because this broad pattern echoes back over recent centuries.

Elsewhere I have argued that it is reasonable to think of three imperial ages of illicit financial flows (Cobham, 2022). Illicit financial flows are defined in the UN system as 'Financial flows that are illicit in origin, transfer or use, that reflect an exchange of value and that cross country borders… A flow of value is considered illicit if it is illicitly generated (e.g. originates from criminal activities or tax evasion), illicitly transferred (e.g. violating currency controls) or illicitly used (e.g. for financing terrorism)' (UNODC & UNCTAD, 2020, p. 12).

Tax-related illicit flows are the largest component, and there are two main common features. First, illicit flows depend on a lack of transparency to go unchallenged; and second, they will tend to undermine the volume of public funds and the quality of governance that directs them. Together this acts to undermine the 4 Rs of tax.

The period of formal European empire (very roughly from the 15th to the mid-20th century) can be considered as the first imperial age of illicit flows. The violent extraction may have been state-led but was unquestionably illegitimate, made possible by force alone. Much of it, too, took the form of illegitimate taxation – both by charter companies like the East India Company, and by colonial administrators.

The revenues may have contributed to the administration costs, but these were not for the benefit of those 'administered', and much was remitted to the imperial capital and/or extracted as private rents (see, e.g., Rodney, 2018, and many of the case studies in Bhambra & McClure, 2022). As the late Mike Davis documented at length, tax often played a specific, exacerbating role under empire in the conversion of El Niño-related weather events into vast episodes of human famine (Davis, 2000). Time and again, Davis finds evidence that colonial populations were left unable to respond to natural (though dramatic) cycles, because of the extent of extraction by taxation immediately before or often even *during* these periods.

The second age of illicit financial flows emerges as formal empire begins to weaken during the early 20th century. Those who had benefited personally and accumulated assets through empire saw a dual threat. On the one hand, the risk of expropriation (in fact, merely re-appropriation) by newly independent former colonies. On the other hand, the possibility of significant taxation of those assets and the associated income streams by the imperial power – where the prospects and reality of European wars had driven a renewed focus on revenue-raising.

The historian Vanessa Ogle refers to the resulting outflow as 'funk money' (that is, money flowing because those controlling it were in a funk, afraid of the possibility of losing it). Ogle (2020, pp. 218–219) highlights the role these funds played in reshaping the international economy:

> a significant share of funds was moved to an emerging system of offshore tax havens. Low-tax jurisdictions offering opportunities to avoid and evade taxation in countries with regular higher tax rates were not new at this point, but, owing to the influx of funds from the imperial and colonial world, expanded significantly during the years of decolonization. In these decades, savvy lawyers and bankers discovered Switzerland, Liechtenstein, Luxembourg, the British Channel Islands and, for the United States, the Bahamas and Bermuda, for the purpose of registering companies and trusts, or just depositing funds in bank accounts in order to benefit from zero or very low tax rates.

Thus began the more deliberate phase of developing 'tax havens', to service and profit from the needs of those with funds to move. The desire to cling onto illicitly gained assets and also to escape imperial taxation was complicated by the recognition that the protection of empire was also necessary to maintain property rights. Jurisdictions under the same crown, and within the same legal system, were therefore particularly attractive (Palan, 2002; Palan et al., 2010) – just as long as they also had sufficient autonomy to set their own tax rules, and their users felt safe from any risk of imperial overreach.

There were also specific conditions that made this argument especially strong in the case of the *British* empire in particular. Such was the power and global extent of the British empire that the familiarity of its laws for the regulation of capital, coupled with common law's ease of use for international commerce (since published judgments dominate, rather than codified statutes as under civil law), is one element (Berkowitz et al., 2003;

Fennell, 2017; Pistor, 2019; Rubin, 1977). Another is the political context of the following decades, including after the 1939–1945 war.

Journalist and author Nicholas Shaxson (2011) writes that it is 'no coincidence that the City of London, once the capital of the greatest empire the world has known, is the center of the most important part of the global offshore system… accounting for about half the world's secrecy jurisdictions. This is a layered hub-and-spoke array of tax havens… which mostly emerged from the ashes of the British empire.'

Shaxson's archival research on the debate inside the British government and financial institutions in the 1950s and 1960s illustrated competing concerns. On one hand were worries over the threat to UK tax revenues. On the other, a hope that dependent territories could become financially self-sustaining, and the opportunity to bolster the City of London.

More detailed work by Kristine Sævold pushes back against a simple view of 'tacit approval' by the British state. Sævold (2022, p. 242) emphasises instead 'the importance of duality, incoherence, postponement, and reluctance to properly account for an emergent and controversial policy area in the context of decolonization and anti-imperialist criticism' – suggesting the British state may never have taken a clear position.

As Sævold shows, the UK did not adopt a formal tax haven policy until 1971. When they did, it seems to have been used as often to approve as to block requests, and by 1977 had been dropped. Around the same time, dependent territories previously referred to in official documents as 'tax havens' had become 'offshore banking centres': 'One tentative explanation is the wider trend in the late 1970s how larger segments of Western capitalist states, including Britain, had by this point normalized the use of tax havens' (p. 240).

In 1979, Margaret Thatcher came to power and a period of radical capital account liberalisation began (that is, removing regulations on cross-border financial flows), in which many of the remaining barriers to 'offshore' were lifted. By the early 1990s, as discussed in the previous section, the explosion in profit shifting by multinationals had begun in earnest. As Figure 3.2 above illustrates, this has its roots in the late 1970s when the first systematic use of tax havens for the purpose can be identified.

While the exact degree, form and timing of British state approval are uncertain, the outcomes are largely known. Table 3.3 shows the extent to which the UK spider's web dominates the global risks of financial secrecy and tax losses due to offshore evasion; and also the global risks of corporate tax abuse and the associated revenue losses.

Table 3.3 The domination of the UK spider's web (% share of global risks and revenue losses for which the UK web is responsible)

	Financial secrecy risks	Revenue losses due to offshore tax abuse	Corporate tax haven risks	Revenue losses due to corporate tax abuse
UK	1.61%	17.47%	3.12%	10.32%
Jersey	1.35%	1.87%	3.89%	1.64%
Guernsey	1.79%	0.57%	2.16%	0.05%
Isle of Man	0.56%	0.17%	1.92%	1.17%
Bermuda	0.72%	1.58%	5.67%	6.25%
BVI	1.83%	3.13%	6.45%	1.87%
Cayman	1.52%	25.64%	5.99%	3.35%
Other BOTs	1.10%	0.04%	2.03%	2.36%
UK Network, total	**10.47%**	**50.48%**	**31.23%**	**27.01%**
Memo: Next biggest threat, after UK	*5.74%*	*11.94%*	*5.54%*	*16.24%*
	(USA)	*(USA)*	*(Netherlands)*	*(Netherlands)*

Note: data from Financial Secrecy Index 2022, Corporate Tax Haven Index 2021 and State of Tax Justice 2023.

The various columns show the responsibilities of each jurisdiction or group. The first column shows values from the Financial Secrecy Index. These are the responsibilities of each jurisdiction, calculated as a share of the global risks of cross-border tax evasion (and other illicit financial flows) that they pose. The second column shows the share of revenue losses to offshore evasion each jurisdiction is estimated to be responsible for. The third and fourth column give similar values in relation to corporate tax abuse, showing respectively each jurisdiction's assessed share of the global risk of facilitating abuse (via the Corporate Tax Haven Index), and of the revenue losses imposed on others.

The UK with its web of dependent territories leads in each category, but is not uniquely responsible. Indeed, many EU and OECD member countries – that is, the former imperial powers and settler states – play a substantial role. While these states and their citizens are the greatest losers in financial terms, it is lower-income countries – former colonies – that bear the most intense costs of the extraction of value that is conducted.

We live, then, in the third imperial age of illicit financial flows: 'tax haven empire', if you will. The period of financial globalisation covering recent decades is characterised by the shift of tax havenry from the periphery to the core.

Simultaneously, cross-border tax abuse has morphed from a marginal activity into one which is material to the global economy, in the accounting sense, due to the trillions of dollars in shifted profit and undeclared incomes. The process not only extracts value through illicit flows. By undermining the tax systems of all countries, and most intensely those of former colonies, it denies the benefits of effective statehood to much of the world's population.

This third imperial age of illicit financial flows can thus be seen as part of a continuing process of extraction, which drives inequalities between countries as well as within them. The research of Ndikumana and Boyce summarised above has demonstrated that the African continent should be seen as a net creditor rather than a net debtor to the world. That is, African countries are owed a debt for what has been extracted – far from the perception that they are borrowers, reliant on debt and aid. Equally, it should be clear that the broader set of former colonies are owed a debt – and one that continues to grow, as long as the international conditions for tax justice are not in place.

The following chapter explores critically the multiple measures for policy reform and institutional overhaul that have been proposed as steps towards tax justice. Progress could finally 'stop the clock' on the continuing growth of the debt owed. More than that, given the role of tax in imperial extraction, there are opportunities to consider how tax could play a reparative role now – a 5th R of tax – in addressing some part of the accumulated debt.

The need for reparative or restorative justice extends not only to those countries and peoples who lose out to tax abuse today. The UK spider's web includes many jurisdictions that have themselves seen violent extraction and enslavement over centuries, and in the most recent period have been facilitated down the road to tax havenry – with further social costs for the majority of their own people too. The UK has a responsibility to consider here, and a role to play financially in supporting the development of alternative economic models. The scale of the threat posed to these jurisdictions by the climate crisis adds particular urgency to the UK's challenge.

The problem of cross-border tax abuse is international, and so must be the solutions. National governments are not powerless, however, and there is much that can still be delivered unilaterally or in regional groupings, and by countries at any given level of per capita income. The following chapter sets out and evaluates both national and international tax justice proposals.

what should we do about tax justice?

The range of measures that have been proposed to support the achievement of tax justice is broad indeed. With some inevitable overlap, these are presented for clarity in three sections. The first addresses financial transparency measures. These include both domestic and international aspects. The key elements can be thought of as necessary steps towards tax justice, although insufficient on their own.

The second section focuses on more narrowly domestic measures, including public disclosures and enforcement questions as well as a range of good taxes and tax approaches. The third section addresses areas where international approaches are needed, including institutional proposals to set the basis for future decision-making also.

Although many of the proposals are necessarily technical in nature, they are fundamentally political in aim. Some allow people to hold tax authorities and governments accountable for applying taxes fairly and effectively. Some empower tax authorities with new tools and information to combat tax abuse by the largest companies and wealthiest households, despite the resources wielded by their professional advisers. And some swing the balance of power in international decision-making, so that all governments can be heard – including by their own people, and the influence of lobbyists is exposed.

Tax is messy, precisely because it's not just technical. It's about how we want to live together as people. There are no perfect answers, and no permanent solutions. Today's fix will be defeated by tomorrow's innovation in tax abuse. The lobbyists and professional enablers of tax abuse won't stop, so neither can the system. That means keeping political attention focused, and making sure the data is available for people and authorities to respond.

It can feel hopeless to see the scale of tax abuse, and the power of those involved. But ultimately, the power to demand better human outcomes rests with all of us in society, and we have the research to know a great deal of what works better.

The ABC of tax transparency

The ABC refers to the three main transparency elements of the policy platform set out by the Tax Justice Network in the early 2000s. A is for the automatic exchange of information on financial accounts. B is for beneficial ownership transparency. C is for public country by country reporting by multinationals.

In each area, longstanding scepticism has given way to broad acceptance, and the ABC now forms part of the global policy agenda. However, none of the three has been delivered in full, nor yet with full inclusion of all countries. The partial delivery does provide a stronger evidence base on the potential value of each element, however, and points to the next steps.

Automatic exchange of information: End bank secrecy

Multilateral, automatic exchange of financial information is the process whereby each year, governments share information with each other on the financial accounts held in their jurisdictions, by tax residents of the other. A Swiss bank, for example, will tell its government that a UK resident has an account with them, which received a certain income in the year, and the Swiss government will let HMRC know so they can reconcile this with the tax return of the person in question. Automatic exchange is the critical tool to overcome the scourge of bank secrecy, and the associated undeclared offshore accounts.

By 2018, more than 100 jurisdictions had signed up to automatic exchange under the OECD Common Reporting Standard (CRS). This includes all the major financial centres except the USA, and in 2021 covered 111 million accounts holding almost €11 trillion (Global Forum on Transparency and Exchange of Information for Tax Purposes, 2022). This was a significant breakthrough. But as will be explored below, most lower-income countries still remain excluded, the United States is in open non-compliance, and there are serious questions over the effectiveness of the system.

Back in the year 2000, information exchange was a niche technical area, with only the very beginnings of public attention. The UK's still new government led by Tony Blair and Gordon Brown published a white paper on globalisation which recognised that opacity about overseas assets including financial accounts 'can offer cover for tax evasion', and committed 'to promote international co-operation in information exchange about taxable income' (HMG, 2000, p.58). The white paper drew on Oxfam's important (2000) study of the cost of tax havens for international development, and a background paper which noted that 'developing country treasuries find it very difficult to tax overseas assets effectively, particularly because they do not enjoy full exchange of information with host countries' (FitzGerald & Cobham, p. 8).

The OECD study released the same year, titled 'Improving Access to Bank Information for Tax Purposes', begins with the clearest possible counter-statement: 'Bank secrecy is widely recognised as playing a legitimate role in protecting the confidentiality of the financial affairs of individuals and legal entities' (p. 7). The report does, nonetheless, recognise the role of opacity in promoting tax evasion.

And while it took more than ten years and a financial crisis in the global North, it was eventually accepted that only automatic exchange could be effective.

The London summit of the G20 countries chaired by UK prime minister Gordon Brown saw a concerted push to require jurisdictions to sign up to TIEAs: OECD Tax Information Exchange Agreements, which formalised arrangements for information exchange upon request, bilaterally. This was supposed to improve the functioning of 'upon request' exchange, since there was still opposition to automatic exchange. But as leading commentator Lee Sheppard (2009) noted later that year, 'The standard OECD information exchange agreement is nearly worthless. Information exchange under the standard agreement is sporadic, difficult, and unwieldy for tax administrators even under the best of circumstances. When a banking haven is the requested party, information exchange is nearly impossible.' Meinzer (2012) laid out in further detail the ways in which secrecy jurisdictions could, and did, stymie any requests they received.

But while the London G20 might not have delivered on its claim to be ending bank secrecy, the narrative shift it reflected and amplified was powerful. As a senator, Barack Obama had helped to introduce a bill attacking bank secrecy in 2008. By 2010, as president, he was signing into law the Foreign Account Tax Compliance Act (FATCA) which required all foreign financial institutions to provide information – automatically – about US tax citizens' accounts.

The most dramatic effect was felt in Switzerland, which had always resisted EU pressure to cooperate with the Savings Directive. Now Swiss banks were lobbying their own government, begging it to create an intergovernmental arrangement for them to collectively provide the information needed – rather than face the risk, individually, of having their access blocked to the biggest market in the world.

The decision to implement FATCA paved the way for the G20 to request the OECD to create a multilateral instrument for automatic information exchange: the Common Reporting Standard or CRS, which initially appeared likely to meet the longstanding demands of campaigners.

While the CRS is multilateral and automatic, it has significant limits. Despite the multilateral umbrella, the arrangements remain bilateral. In other words, each pair of signatories must still agree to provide information to each other, even though they have both signed up to the instrument already. Following the Obama administration's U-turn on participation (Cobham, 2014), before the standard was even finalised, the OECD sought to recognise that its biggest member would only provide reciprocal information under certain conditions, in a small number of the intergovernmental arrangements that it negotiated.

As a result, the CRS allows each signatory to decide which other signatory jurisdictions it will exchange information with. Switzerland and many others followed the US example and simply refused to activate exchange relationships with many other signatories. Disappointingly but unsurprisingly, researchers find evidence to support the hypothesis 'that secrecy jurisdictions purposefully refrain from activating AIE relationships with countries to which they supply secrecy'. In addition, the most powerful (OECD) countries are able to insist on information exchange from the secrecy jurisdictions that pose the greatest threat to them – but lower-income signatories remain exposed (Janský et al., 2022).

Lower-income countries are also largely excluded even from becoming signatories. Harking back to old narratives on bank secrecy, the OECD introduced a criterion for participation around confidentiality. Countries could only become signatories if they could reach a set of technical thresholds around the protection of data received. The practical effect has been to create a bar for participation, whereby willing countries cannot become members if they do not have a high degree of administrative and technical infrastructure, and a government willing to prioritise this area above others that may well be more urgent.

The OECD CRS also requires reciprocity from all signatories. While this is a welcome goal, it seems ludicrous to demand that a low-income country like Malawi should invest in systems for confidentiality, and to be able to provide information on the bank accounts of Swiss tax residents, for example, before Malawi itself can receive any information. In fact, Malawi could potentially make the investment and jump through the OECD hoops, only to find that when they are able to join the CRS, neither Switzerland nor any other signatory is even willing to provide them with information.

Each year, the OECD provides information to be published in the UN Financing Sustainable Development Report. Each year, the data show that lower-income countries continue to be largely excluded from the CRS. The 2022 report shows 112 signatories, of which 37 are middle-income countries (out of a possible 108), and eight are African states (out of a possible 54) (IATF, 2022).[1]

At the technical level, there remain concerns over the ability of the CRS to respond to threats from professional enablers of abuse (e.g. Khadjavi & Vertelman, 2022; Morris, 2017; Noked, 2018). This is illustrated by a less high-profile story to emerge in the Suisse Secrets leak. The bank apparently promoted layered ownership arrangements to hold bank accounts, including trusts and holding companies with Credit Suisse staff as nominees, which would defeat CRS reporting because the true owner would not be directly identified in order for information to be passed to the home country tax authority (OCCRP & Süddeutsche Zeitung, 2022).

So-called 'golden visas' (schemes in which jurisdictions sell citizenship or residence, typically in exchange for commitments of investment) also remain a threat, since they create the possibility of misdirecting information under exchange away from the tax authorities of the true tax residence. That is, if you register with the bank as a (tax-paying) citizen of Cyprus, they will not exchange information with your actual tax authority in Argentina, say.

Research indicates that the CRS has been effective but remains vulnerable to growing exploitation of such loopholes. Using data up to 2019, Ahrens, Hakelberg and Rixen (2022) find evidence of small but growing use of golden visa schemes and of the exploitation of schemes to hide beneficial ownership such as through trusts. They conclude: 'Overall, our results suggest that regulatory arbitrage is not yet widespread, but it seems to increase over time.'

---

1 Middle-income total from World Bank, https://datahelpdesk.worldbank.org/knowledgebase/articles/906519-world-bank-country-and-lending-groups (accessed 28.3.2023).

Langenmayr and Zyska (2023) explore this effect from the other side. They consider the example of a German taxpayer who buys Dominican citizenship and uses this to open a Swiss bank account. The data would show an increase in Dominica's bank deposits in a secrecy jurisdiction. Analysis reveals a consistent increase in cross-border bank deposits of this type after a country starts to offer golden visas, which is fully consistent with a tax evasion motivation.

The biggest single weakness of CRS as it stands, however, is the continuing refusal of the biggest single financial centre (and OECD member) to reciprocate. As Lukas Hakelberg (2020) writes in *The Hypocritical Hegemon*, 'the United States exploited widespread compliance with [automatic information exchange] by refusing to participate itself. Therefore, the country currently enjoys an almost exclusive competitive advantage in the attraction of hidden capital' (p. 83).

Analysis at the jurisdiction level indicates that the major effect of the introduction of the CRS was not a drop in cross-border bank deposits, but a redistribution: away from financial centres that signed up, and towards the US. Casi et al. (2020) find a reduction in cross-border bank deposits in 'tax havens' of $45 billion, as a lower bound; but an increase in US cross-border deposits of $55 billion. This is consistent with the ECORYS (2021) study cited in the previous chapter, showing no impact of CRS on the estimated volume of undeclared offshore assets.

The basic elements are now in place – above all, recognition of the need for multilateral, automatic information exchange to defeat the tax evasion and other crimes that bank secrecy makes possible. What is lacking is to ensure that the system is effective and inclusive of all countries. Narrowly, that requires a concerted effort to close loopholes and to recognise that this will be an ongoing process, to keep up with those who will seek to circumvent transparency.

But the bigger shift needed is to establish the principle of true multilateralism in the process. That includes requiring that all signatories exchange information with each other, not only some favoured subgroup. It means supporting all countries to become signatories, rather than throwing up roadblocks. And it means having an effective means to discipline those who refuse to participate – even, or rather especially, where that is the largest financial centre in the world. It is in theory possible for the OECD to achieve these aims. But as we will see below, the growing momentum for an international tax cooperation framework under UN auspices points the way to a structure and process that is much more likely to be able to meet these goals for inclusivity and fair dealing.

The potential benefits are great. The Internal Revenue Service of the US has conducted the most comprehensive comparison of compliance under different conditions of information availability. The key finding relates to the propensity for taxpayers to misreport their income, depending on whether or not there are alternative information sources on that income. In short, if taxpayers know that authorities have another source of information on their income, they are seven times more likely to declare correctly themselves (Black et al., 2012). Taxpayers misreport their income by *more than half* when there is no other source of information available; while the simple existence of alternative information reduces that misreporting by 85%.

Now think of the estimated $169 billion of tax revenue lost due to undeclared offshore income: the potential returns on comprehensive automatic information exchange would exceed $140 billion *each year*. In contrast, the Global Forum (2022) identifies €114 billion of additional revenues *in total*, not annually, some of which does not relate to automatic exchange. The CRS's lack of inclusiveness and effectiveness means that the major revenue gains remain unclaimed.

Beneficial ownership transparency: End anonymous ownership

Anonymous ownership is at the heart of most tax evasion, and most other illicit financial flows. For companies, trusts, foundations, partnerships and other legal vehicles and arrangements, as the Financial Action Task Force (the global anti-money-laundering body, based at the OECD) puts it, 'their unique legal status lends them to be used in complex schemes designed to conceal the true beneficial owners and, in many respects, the real reason for holding assets and conducting transactions. Corporate vehicles can be misused for various illicit purposes, including money laundering, bribery and corruption, insider dealings, tax fraud, terrorist financing, sanctions evasion and other illegal activities' (FATF, 2023).

The longstanding demand of campaigners for public registration of beneficial owners made a breakthrough in 2013 when it was adopted onto the policy agenda of the G8 group of countries, in the year it was chaired by UK prime minister David Cameron. Progress has been slow, however, and recently suffered a significant reverse.

There are three key elements to end anonymous ownership in this way (Knobel, 2019a). First, jurisdictions that allow the creation of legal vehicles with the power to hold assets or generate income should require registration of up-to-date information on the beneficial ownership. That means, specifically, identifying the warm-blooded human being/s who benefit from and/or make decisions for the legal vehicle in question. This prevents people hiding ownership by layering it in further structures, in the same or other jurisdictions.

Second, the registers should be fully online and freely available to the public. This allows everyone to know who they are doing business with, or competing with, for example. Markets work better, just as tax and regulation work better, when anonymity is not possible.

And third, the information in the registers must be high quality. That means the data needs to be verified and up to date, with meaningful penalties for failure, and no egregious loopholes (such as very high thresholds, so that owners with less than 25% of shares need not register). Verification requires validation against other, often confidential administrative datasets (e.g. from tax authorities and financial intelligence units, FIUs). Figure 4.1 illustrates the public and private elements of the process.

Registers such as that for UK companies have proven pivotal in uncovering major corruption, including multiple 'laundromat' schemes (major money-laundering schemes that typically involve large volumes of dirty money, multiple banks and cover many jurisdictions: the famous 'Russian Laundromat' uncovered by OCCRP (2014) identified more than $20 billion laundered through almost 100 jurisdictions). But the UK register still lacks robust verification and instead demonstrates daily the ease of abuse. Those registered by the UK's Companies House as bona fide beneficial owners include Mr Xxx Stalin and Mr Mmmmmm Xxxxxxxxxxx (Bullough, 2019). Much more serious is the freedom to insert, unverified, the details of real people into real companies. A common issue is with 'burner' companies, set up to obtain fraudulent loans. Successful scams of this type leave people entirely unaware that their names and addresses have been used until demands for repayment start to arrive (Hussain & Davies, 2022).

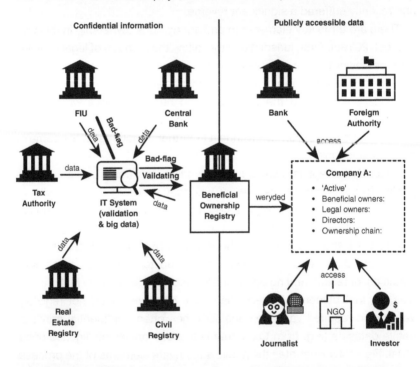

Figure 4.1 Verification and validation of public beneficial ownership data

Source: Knobel (2019a), Figure 8.

With the UK failing behind, the EU had led the way in recent years, introducing registers for trusts as well as companies under various anti-money-laundering directives. However, 2022 saw a major setback as the EU Court of Justice ruled that the registers constituted a breach of the human right to privacy.

The claimant in the case made an argument commonly heard from opponents of ownership transparency, that 'disclosure of that information would expose him and his family, in a way that is distinct, genuine and current, to "disproportionate risk, risk of fraud, kidnapping, blackmail, extortion, harassment, violence or intimidation"' (On Behalf of WM, 2020). One of the lawyers who led the appeal for Mishcon de Reya of London welcomed the decision as 'a victory for data protection and the Rule of Law', after 'high-profile public campaigns run by highly organised and single-minded transparency campaigners [had] succeeded in stymying the debate about ends and means, and the principle of proportionality, which is at the core of the Rule of Law' (Mishcon de Reya, 2022). In this way, the lawyers framed the case explicitly as a victory against transparency, and the judgment seems to confirm that individual secrecy about the ownership and control of legal entities was the dominant concern.

Opposing human rights claims were not, however, put forward to the court by the defendant, the Luxembourg business register. These could have highlighted the human rights costs of continuing to allow anonymous ownership, including through the undermining of the 4 Rs of tax (see, e.g., Nelson, 2021). They could also have shown how the claimant approached their own concerns over privacy. A prolific user of social media, the claimant regularly advertised his and his family's international travel, very often their current location, and his apparently substantial wealth. In addition, investigative journalists quickly uncovered that the claimant 'has been the owner or director of over 110 companies registered in countries around the world, including well-known secrecy havens like Belize, the British Virgin Islands, and Luxembourg', including a number with politically connected Russian directors (Peco et al., 2023). Others noted that Mishcon de Reya itself had only recently paid a major fine in the UK for 'serious breaches' of anti-money-laundering rules (Siddique & Davies, 2022),

Following the case, many EU members withdrew public access to their beneficial ownership registers. Others, including in UK dependent territories, announced that they would consider whether to move ahead with their own (often reluctant) commitments to introduce public registers. The Financial Action Task Force (FATF) continues to require private rather than public registers as part of its relevant standard (FATF recommendation 24). The US – the major member, which often controls the pace of progress – is moving towards the introduction of a private register. There is no doubt though that momentum towards transparency has suffered a major setback, and opponents have been given a major boost by the court ruling. European policymakers are now considering their next steps.

Away from the court case, there is a less commonly heard but more powerful human rights argument around the scope for beneficial ownership registration to become a vehicle for establishing ownership rights of the powerful, rather than of the rightful. Powerfully documented cases of land dispossession range from rural communities in Scotland (Wightman's *The Poor Had No Lawyers*, 2010), to 'non-Europeans with no economic power (indigenous, enslaved black people, mestizos and women)' across Latin America historically (GRAIN, 2022) and continuing in the present abuses of agribusinesses (GRAIN, 2020), to communities descended from West African people enslaved to work on cotton farms in Florida in the US (Brown, 2023).

If there is a human rights challenge to public registers of beneficial ownership to take seriously, it is this one. A system that creates exclusive property rights, in effect, is inevitably open to unjust claims of the more powerful – those with lawyers, that is. But this demands not that we accept anonymous ownership, and all the tax abuse and other corrupt practices that it enables. Instead, it calls for an awareness of the political as well as the technical: that it can never be enough to introduce a transparency 'solution', without a clear eye on questions of power. Who will record their ownership? What obstacles exist? How can power imbalances be addressed, rather than locked in? If anything, however, this concern emphasises the crucial need for the information to be fully public – so that illicit claims can be seen and contested in real time, rather than after the 'fact'.

More broadly, it is clear that ending anonymous ownership is an important goal to prevent private abuse, at the expense of social benefits. Markets, states and societies work better when we all know who we are dealing with. Taking this agenda forward, over the sustained opposition of powerful supporters of opacity, must ensure that the benefits are fully shared. The proposal for a global asset registry discussed below provides the basis to consider comprehensive transparency of ownership, and an opportunity to agree ambitious standards.

Country-by-country reporting: Make multinationals tax-transparent

The third element of the ABC of tax transparency relates to multinationals and aims to put them on a level playing field for transparency with standalone domestic businesses that publish annual accounts. The consolidated, global accounts of multinationals require little in the way of national-level data. The separate accounts of their subsidiary entities, meanwhile, require little if any disaggregation of intragroup and external transactions. Requirements even to publish the names and jurisdictions of subsidiaries and joint ventures are patchy at best.

While the accounts of domestic businesses provide a relatively clear picture of the scale of economic activity, profits made and tax paid, at the level of individual countries, the accounts of multinationals simply do not. Country-by-country reporting is designed as the simplest set of data that can address this.

The idea goes back to discussions at the United Nations that aimed to establish a degree of accountability for multinationals outside of their headquarters countries, for broader reasons than tax alone (Cobham et al., 2018). Early conversations as the Tax Justice Network was being formed gave rise to the publication of a draft international accounting standard that became the basis of campaigning in the extractive sector at first and then more generally (Christensen, 2012; Cobham et al., 2017; Murphy, 2003).

Ten years later, in 2013, and with corporate tax abuse a growing concern, the G20 group of countries cut through the opposition of the big four accounting firms (who had stalled a draft standard for the extractives sector at the International Accounting Standards Board), and directed the OECD to produce a standard for all large multinationals.

The resulting OECD standard closely resembled the original Tax Justice Network standard, except in three main regards. First, the drafting was loose in important areas so that certain variables are ill-defined or defined without consistency with accounting standards (of which group profit is the most egregious). Second, some significant variables were dropped altogether, under pressure (most importantly, wages and all intra-group transactions with the exception of sales). A high size threshold was also introduced so that only multinationals with a turnover consistently above €750,000 would be required to report.

Third, in the area where resistance focused most strongly, the OECD did not propose that the data be made public. Worse, rather than allowing each tax authority where a multinational has operations to access the data directly, the OECD created a complex set of information exchange arrangements under which other countries' tax authorities could only receive data from the headquarters country tax authority, where the multinational would file the data.

Since the standard was introduced in 2015, for reporting from the 2016 financial year onwards, there has been growing pressure for the OECD to address each of these points – including from multinationals like Vodafone that voluntarily publish their reporting data, and who have highlighted the discrepancy between the profits data and the more accurate number in their accounts.

Notwithstanding these concerns, the introduction of country-by-country reporting had important impacts. Even for private reporting to headquarters country tax authorities only, research found a 1–2 percentage point increase in the effective tax rates firms paid, and evidence of a decline in profit shifting (Joshi, 2020). Where firms' effective tax rates are typically under 20 percentage points, this implies a 5–10% increase or more in revenues.

The EU also introduced more limited forms of country-by-country reporting for banks and for the extractive sector in the same period, and despite their technical flaws these had the advantage of requiring public disclosure. For banks, research shows a significant decline in tax haven use compared to non-disclosing insurance firms (Eberhartinger et al., 2020); and a fall of effective tax rates, for banks that use tax havens most, of 3.6 percentage points (Overesch & Wolff, 2021).

This evidence suggests that, at worst, making the data public would likely double the benefits of the OECD standard in reducing corporate tax abuse – as well as reducing compliance costs for both reporting companies and tax authorities. But the resistance to transparency remains. Despite repeated denials, the OECD was recently exposed as having lobbied the Australian government to reverse its electoral commitment to start publishing the data (Agyemang, 2023).

In lieu of full publication, the OECD began to publish aggregate statistics on the country-by-country reporting data. These are not company-level data, but provide the aggregate position for all multinationals from a given country – so, for example, it is possible to see the collective position of US multinationals in Ireland, in France, in Cayman and so on. As discussed in the previous chapter, these data allowed the first broadly comprehensive, global estimates to be made to the scale and nature of profit shifting. That, in turn, has contributed to the growing understanding that current tax rules under the arm's-length principle simply cannot and will not align profits with the location of real activity; and a clearer public view of just how bad that misalignment is.

Meanwhile, voluntary measures continued to gain momentum. The Fair Tax Foundation had launched in the UK in 2014, with a Fair Tax Mark that companies could obtain if they met the criteria, to demonstrate to the public that they met appropriate standards for tax and transparency. For multinationals, the standard could be met largely by publishing their country-by-country reporting data, and this allowed early adopters such as SSE, a major energy company listed on the FTSE100 and which obtained the mark in 2014, to provide a lead to others.

Throughout 2018 and 2019, the Global Reporting Initiative (GRI, the leading setter of sustainability standards worldwide) explored proposals to introduce a tax standard. A technical committee with expert representatives from labour, investors, reporting companies, the big four accountants, academia and civil society was created and produced a draft standard. Following extensive consultation and trialling, the new standard Tax: 207 was adopted, with a public launch in 2020 and coming into effect for reporting in 2021.

The GRI standard addresses every weakness of the OECD standard, providing for comprehensive country-by-country reporting and combining this with rigorous tax policy commitments for reporting companies. A growing number of companies from Vodafone and Philips to Shell and Rio Tinto have adopted the voluntary standard, and in addition the GRI standards are required for listed companies by many stock markets around the world.

In 2020, the OECD held a public consultation and received highly aligned responses from civil society, independent experts and – importantly – from investors with trillions of dollars of assets under management. An analysis of the average responses on key points, for different types of submitting organisation, showed that investors called overwhelmingly for the weaknesses of the OECD approach to be addressed by simply converging to the GRI standard, and requiring the data to be public so that all stakeholders can benefit (Tax Justice Network, 2020). Opposition was largely restricted to multinational lobby groups and professional services firms including the big four accounting firms who make large profits from selling tax advice.

Three years later, and despite the clarity of the response – or perhaps because of precisely that – the OECD has still not reached a conclusion on its own public consultation.

The Fair Tax Foundation has since launched a variant of its Mark focused specifically on global multinationals, including those operating outside of the UK. Take-up of the GRI standard, which is also consistent with the Fair Tax Mark, has continued to grow. And investors have become increasingly active. Working with civil society and the labour movement, they have pushed shareholders in companies like Amazon and Cisco at their annual general meetings to debate and vote on publishing their country-by-country reporting, coming surprisingly close to success a number of times. In addition, investors have been clearly heard by the US Stock Exchange Commission which is considering whether to join other stock markets and make publication of GRI standard data a requirement for US listing.

Elsewhere, the EU is already committed to require publication of the company-level data for operations in EU member states at least, and some 'high-risk' other countries. Australia has committed to introduce full public reporting but not yet brought forward the legislation. The Financial Accounting Standards Board in the US has just required that companies publish jurisdiction-level tax data quarterly and annually, and the next step is to seek jurisdiction-level activity data to set alongside. The sense is growing that full public reporting with more or less global coverage is now close. The more difficult question may turn out to be how quickly the robust GRI standard can be confirmed as the common basis. A remaining question is whether the OECD can maintain a role here, or if – as seems increasingly likely – it will be left behind by more ambitious countries *and* companies acting unilaterally.

The ABC of tax transparency has been on quite a journey. When the Tax Justice Network combined these elements in its original policy platform in 2003–2005, each was seen by policymakers and OECD experts as unrealistic, at best utopian and at worst a type of fool's gold, destined to waste energy and detract from tangible progress. By 2013, however, each element had been brought onto the global policy agenda at the G8 and G20 groups of countries. The OECD had been given a mandate to introduce both automatic exchange and country-by-country reporting, while the UK and others had begun to move forward directly on public registers of beneficial ownership.

Arguably, the ABC is a major success story for advocacy, research and campaigning by the global movement. But we remain a long way short. Automatic exchange is beset by loopholes and excludes most lower-income countries, and is roundly ignored by the biggest financial centre, the United States. Beneficial ownership transparency remains only partly in place, mainly for companies and lacking for most other entities in most jurisdictions. Country-by-country reporting is firmly established but not yet with effective access for lower-income countries or the public, while convergence to the GRI standard would improve the quality significantly and also reduce compliance costs.

The returns to full introduction of the ABC are of course uncertain, but in each case likely to be very large indeed. But the resistance to transparency, including the active opposition of the professional enablers of tax abuse and too often of the OECD itself, has held up progress in the last ten years. In addition, the intermediating role of the OECD has resulted in the benefits of the measures, as introduced, being systematically biased against lower-income countries.

A key question for tax justice in the next decade is whether the OECD can be forced to overcome its own biases, or whether the only viable progress now is through the process to create an international tax body under UN auspices.

Domestic measures

Two key supporting planks of the domestic policy agenda add the DE of tax justice to the ABC: *disclosure* and *enforcement*. Together they are crucial to ensuring that taxes are applied fairly, and are perceived to be so by the wider public. That in turn underpins the degree of tax morale, and tax compliance, without which the social contract can quickly unravel. A third area of measures for tax justice concerns the type of taxes that are even considered as part of the standard policy set.

Disclosure: Let people see tax justice being done

It is important that we can see tax justice in action. Public confidence that all taxpayers are being treated fairly, and that the system as a whole is progressive and effective, is crucial for the role of tax in building the social contract. It also underpins tax morale, and the willingness of everyone to pay their own taxes. That requires, at a minimum, disclosures of aggregate statistics on the tax authority and its performance.

Best practice starts with consistent, aggregate performance measures of the tax authority itself. This area combines elements that build accountability and public confidence in the authority, and also provide the basis for broader accountability of the government over its tax and related policy positions. A second area of corporate disclosures relates to tax behaviour and broader corporate accountability, including as an important indicator of respect for human rights.

Authority disclosures can provide consistent data on the performance and integrity of the tax system and its operation, and on the policy stance of governments in key areas. Research confirms the importance of transparency to support compliance, perhaps most strongly through building taxpayer trust (Adeyeye & Otusanya, 2015; Al-Maghrebi et al., 2022; Siahaan, 2013).

Basic data on revenue-raising – which taxes raise how much? – must be complemented by more detailed data on the distributional implications. Which households contribute, and to what degree, to each type of tax? This necessarily entails the publication of consistent data on the nature of wealth and income inequalities. A statement of the greater share of income tax paid by the highest-income households in the UK, for example, has little meaning without data on the (sharper) increase in those households' share of total income.

Figure 4.2 shows the income tax position for UK households at the 90th percentile – that is, the point at which households enter the richest 10%. The thick black line shows how this group's income has stretched away from the national midpoint. The 90th percentile's income has grown from around 180% of median income in 1990, to over 220% by 2022. At the same time, however, the share paid in income tax followed a downward trend over the period, indicating the system becoming less progressive if anything as inequality rose. (The period from the late 1990s to the early 2010s, roughly coinciding with the Blair–Brown governments, is somewhat different. The rise in income share tailed off, and the tax rate increased gradually until the onset of the financial crisis in 2008. But the broad patterns hold over the whole period.)

Distributional data is also important to contribute to informed public debate on the balance between more and less progressive taxes, and to raise the salience of indirect taxes like VAT that are borne most intensely by lower-income households. Best practice includes a breakdown by income decile and gender for the incidence of each tax, as well as overall statistics on the taxes borne by each. The UK publishes substantial data of this form, providing a model for others, but can go further.

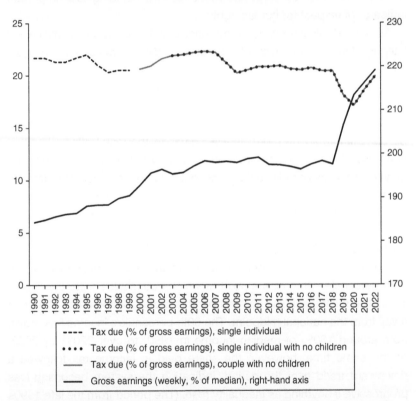

Figure 4.2 The falling tax contribution of the UK's top 10%, as they pull away from the median

Source: author calculations from Annual Survey of Hours and Earnings data (Table 2.7: Income tax (net of tax credits) as a per cent of gross earnings for specimen families). Note: graph shows the earnings (relative to the median household) and the tax rate of UK households at the 90th percentile.

In addition, data on the relative tax positions of racialised and other-wise marginalised groups is necessary to understand how the tax system ameliorates, or exacerbates, the overlapping inequalities in societies. A study by Decolonising Economics (2022) finds that UK households with a 'White British' head are around nine times as likely to be in the top quintile of total wealth as those of 'Black African' ethnicity and 18 times as likely as those of Bangladeshi ethnicity. The percentage of households with financial debts that exceed their financial assets was highest for the Black African and Other Asian groups (both 44%), and twice as likely for these households compared with the White British group. How should the tax system respond? A key element is to introduce disclosures that capture how the tax system actually affects these and overlapping inequalities, including those based on gender.

As Dorothy Brown's (2021) work highlights in the US case, the tax system can very easily contribute to deepen racial inequalities – inadvertently or not. The same patterns occur all around the world, including with respect to indigenous peoples. Women-headed households are consistently more likely to be in lower-income deciles, as are households including people with disabilities and LGBT people. Because the overlaps of these inequalities are especially deep, and because these same groups are also disproportionately likely to go 'uncounted' for the purposes of accessing public services, a tax system that is 'blind' to these character-istics will almost inevitably worsen the situation (Cobham, 2019). Refusing to collate or publish data on the racialised characteristics of groups in the tax system, for example, will not lead to a productively 'neutral' approach – rather, experience shows it will continue to draw a veil over policies that systematically lead to more unequal outcomes. Would public debate and the resultant policy be better or worse if we knew for a fact, rather than only being able to speculate, that households in the ethnolinguistic groups with the lowest average incomes and wealth tend to pay the highest mar-ginal tax rates overall?

Disclosures relating to policy stance are necessary to ensure public and parliamentary scrutiny. The public should know the cost of individual taxes and tax expenditures (tax breaks and incentives given to particular sectors, companies or types of taxpayer), which are often much more opaque than any other aspect of the allocation of public funds. They are also very large. Researchers at the Global Tax Expenditures Database project show that, for countries at each level of per capita income where they have been able to compile data across 1990–2020, the group average value of expenditures ranges between around 18% and 28% of tax revenues (Aliu et al., 2022). For the UK, GTED (2023) reports forgone revenue of £172 billion in 2020, exceeding 8% of GDP (and around a fifth of tax revenues). Any other public expenditure at that level would be subject to sharply higher scrutiny – but somehow because it is tax, and perhaps because it is 'technical', there is no such consistent disclosure or debate.

Disclosure should include the specific provisions and costs of tax incentives of all types, the cost–benefit analysis supporting their introduction and continued use, and the beneficiaries. As with public procurement, receiving corporate tax incentives is an allocation of public funds for specific policy purposes, and should carry the expectation of full transparency both to ensure effectiveness and to manage the risks of corruption. As the LuxLeaks and LuxLetters illustrate all too well, this must include full publication of tax rulings and any equivalent correspondence with taxpayers or their professional advisers, broadly defined in order to curb the opportunities for jurisdictions to facilitate abuse.

The continuing and shameful provision of tax incentives to fossil fuel extraction – that is, the use of public funds to shorten the time for which the Earth provides us all with a viable living space – should also be an urgent topic for disclosure and debate. In line with indicators of the Financial Secrecy Index and Corporate Tax Haven Index, this should include the full publication of contracts with extractive sector companies.

Other corporate disclosures include the basic responsibilities to publish annual accounts, which for multinationals should include country-by-country reporting. An important element of this, included in the GRI standard, is the disclosure of uncertain tax positions – that is, amounts in dispute or subject to challenge by tax authorities. To address tax abuse, and demonstrate accountability, tax authorities should disclose related data on their own aggregate performance in respect to corporate and individual non-payment of tax.

In respect of corporate tax abuse, this entails aggregate data showing the scale of the 'misalignment' for companies that declare less profit in the country than they should. This provides a metric for the scale of losses and allows the authority to track and demonstrate progress over time. Showing the partner jurisdictions to which profits are shifted can also support accountability for their role (this and a related measure on offshore evasion are proposed in Cobham & Jansky, 2020, Ch. 6).

There would be a value also to the parallel publication of data on companies declaring *more* profit in the country than would be expected. For jurisdictions that themselves facilitate profit shifting (such as the UK), this adds to the accountability and provides again a basis to track and demonstrate progress – in this case, progress in reducing the losses imposed on others.

Equivalent measures have been proposed for offshore tax evasion. Tax authorities participating in the OECD Common Reporting Standard and/or other means of information exchange can publish aggregate data by jurisdiction on the value of accounts and income declared under information exchange, and on the aggregate values declared by taxpayers in their tax returns. This again identifies a series of overall and jurisdiction-level gaps, which can help to guide policy responses and also demonstrate progress over time (a detailed template for public reporting of data from automatic information exchange has been proposed by Knobel & Meinzer, 2017).

Publication of similar data by countries including Germany and Australia has also contributed to international accountability efforts (see Knobel, 2020a and 2020b). This aggregate data on cross-border deposits allows comparison with statistics reported by banks and published as national-level aggregates by the Bank for International Settlements. This data is already used in bilateral estimates of offshore holdings and, combining with national disclosures from Germany and others, can allow the identification of anomalies that may point at tax abuse, and can also help third countries to assess the extent of their own risks.

Additional disclosures relate more directly to enforcement and are discussed in the following section. Overall, while disclosure is not an area that has typically excited either researchers or activists, we should consider it in the 'boring but important' category: these are significant measures to build confidence and effectiveness of our tax systems and our tax morale over time.

Enforcement

Enforcement is critical to the actual and perceived fairness of tax systems. Evidence shows that it not only reduces revenue losses to tax abuse directly, but also 'has an additional and indirect effect on tax compliance through tax morale' (Filippin et al., 2013, p. 320). Further disclosures here are necessary both to support public trust and to ensure accountability of policymakers and officials. Central to effective tax enforcement, however, is a well-resourced and operationally independent tax authority – which, sadly, cannot be taken for granted in any country.

TADAT, the Tax Administration Diagnostic Assessment Tool, was developed by the International Monetary Fund and aid donor countries like the UK and leading EU members, and provides one view of the technical requirements for tax authorities. While the nine key 'performance outcome areas' (POAs) for tax authorities focus on efficiency in areas of tax authority delivery, it is notable that none address either the resourcing or the independence of tax authorities.

The nine POAs in full are: integrity of the registered taxpayer base; effective risk management; supporting voluntary compliance; timely filing of tax declarations; timely payment of taxes; accurate reporting in declarations; effective tax dispute resolution; efficient revenue management; and accountability and transparency.

The main partner countries for TADAT, meanwhile, have been among those responsible for the greatest cuts to their own tax authories. As the European Federation of Public Services Unions (EPSU) reported in 2020, EU authorities (including the UK) had cut 100,000 jobs in their tax authorities between 2008 and 2018, amounting to one in seven of those previously employed (Fulton, 2020). The US, too, saw sharp cuts since 2010 which are only now being partially reversed.

'Austerity' after the financial crisis that began in 2008 provided political cover to cut resources of tax authorities and other relevant agencies (and often their independence too), and this remains a key threat to effective and accountable taxation. The effect of limiting the independence or the resources of tax authorities is never to weaken it randomly, or across the board. Instead, the damage introduces systematic biases. Audit rates and legal enforcement fall for the largest companies and wealthiest households as enforcement weakens, with disproportionate revenue costs and a sharply less progressive overall outcome.

A report from the Government Accountability Office shows that audit rates in the US fell for all groups since 2010. Overall, the audit rate dropped from 0.9% to 0.25% in 2019. But for the highest-income group, earning more than $5 million, the drop was far more dramatic. Audit rates of 16% in 2010 (which were fully justified by the return) fell to just 2% by 2019. The GAO attributes these and other clear reductions in the tax authority's ability to deliver fair and effective service to the 22% cut in resources over the period (CBO, 2020; GAO, 2022).

Evidence for the UK shows that being audited has dynamic benefits that exceed the immediate return (Advani et al., 2023). Individuals who have been audited change their tax behaviour over the following five years (or more), and this explains 60–65% of the overall increase in revenue. By comparing individuals' behaviour across audited and unaudited income types, the researchers demonstrate that the effects are best explained not by increased fear of audit but by the fact that audits create new information at a point in time which constrains future misreporting.

In other words, the process of audit creates a context in which the taxpayer's future behaviour is better, not from fear of being audited again but simply because of the knowledge that the tax authority has access to additional information on their financial position. This is consistent with the large impact of third-party income reporting noted for compliance with US taxes.

Tax administration is tax policy, as the saying has it. It is the most false of all false economies to cut the resources of tax authorities in order to 'save' public funds. Reducing audits on the highest earners will have immediate *and* longer-term revenue costs well in excess of any saving. Those forgone revenues will also covertly reduce the degree of redistribution, making the tax system less progressive without any explicit democratic mandate to do so.

Just enforcement can mean a number of practical actions. These include disclosures to demonstrate the levels of overall resourcing (budgets and staffing), and also delivery and outcome data. These should include rates of audit at each strata of income and wealth (so that it is clear for example if resources are being badly targeted at lower-income, lower-risk taxpayers), as well as estimated rates of compliance across tax type, plus the aggregate statistics detailed above.

A related area concerns public access to tax court rulings. While access to court verdicts is considered a fundamental element of a representative and accountable state, tax courts are typically highly secretive: 80% of jurisdictions assessed in the 2022 Financial Secrecy Index received a score of near or total secrecy. Preventing this access stops the public seeing the application of tax law in practice; obstructs empirical research; and leaves open the possibility of sweetheart deals for large taxpayers, or other forms of corruption in the system (Tax Justice Network, 2022).

Enforcement also rests on the availability of, and access to, accurate and timely information about the ownership of personal and corporate assets and income streams, for which the ABC of tax transparency remains essential. Following from established business and human rights principles, states cannot hope to meet the duty to protect against abuses without fair and effective enforcement – including against the professional enablers and intermediaries of abuse. It is incumbent upon states to ensure a well-resourced tax authority.

The risk of 'state capture' must also be addressed here. Multiple case studies show how corporates use cooperation agreements, memorandums of understanding and intelligence sharing initiatives to capture and unduly influence governments, particularly where the agencies have limited capacity and rely on the 'goodwill' of the very industries being regulated to uphold compliance within the industry. The tobacco industry is a key perpetrator, for example (Snyckers, 2020). Disclosures of all such agreements are necessary to ensure both fair enforcement and public confidence in it.

Finally, and importantly, the opportunities for enforcement are significantly enhanced by the progress that has already been made on the transparency elements of the tax justice agenda. In work originally pioneered for the High-Level Panel on Illicit Financial Flows out of Africa, researchers with the Tax Justice Network have developed a granular approach to assess a jurisdiction's vulnerability to risks of illicit flows in each element of their bilateral economic and financial relationships, looking across all partner jurisdictions (AU/ECA, 2015, Annex IV; Cobham et al., 2019; Cobham et al., 2021). This allows authorities to identify the flows and transactions of greatest risk in each of their commodity trade, banking, portfolio investment and direct investment relationships with other jurisdictions.

This approach is built upon purely public data. It also forms the basis of a growing number of direct partnerships with tax authorities and other agencies, within which private, transaction-level data can be used to achieve a much more specific analysis which, in turn, supports a finely targeted response.

Figure 4.3 shows simple maps for the UK's vulnerability in its outward banking relationships, and Ghana's vulnerability in its outward foreign direct investment. At this broader level, this analysis allows authorities to focus their limited resources on the relationships most likely to be subject to abuse (the UK should worry more about its banking relationships with Cayman than with Ireland, for example). When combined with administrative-level data in a subsequent stage, authorities are able to focus enforcement actions precisely on the actors and transactions of highest risk.

Overall, the enforcement picture is substantially improved over the last two decades, because of the substantial improvement in data availability – often through policies championed by the tax justice

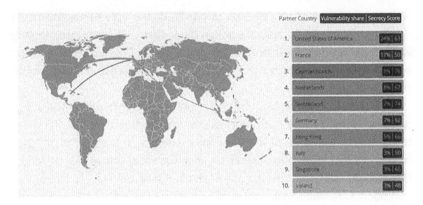

a. UK, outward banking positions

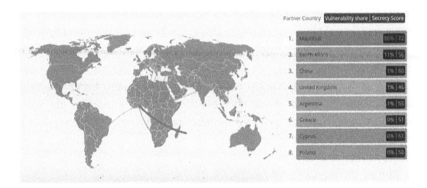

b. Ghana, outward FDI

Figure 4.3 Vulnerability to illicit financial flows

Source: Tax Justice Network (http://iff.taxjustice.net).

movement. But there remains a lack of attention or policy prioritisation for the principle of effective, well-resourced and operationally independent tax authorities. Only with greater public attention, and the development of coherent principles of good practice in this space (what share of revenues, or GDP, constitutes sufficient resourcing for a tax authority and what is best practice in terms of the degree of operational independence, and to limit the scope for harmful political intervention?), are we likely to see consistent improvements around the world.

Good taxes

'Good' taxes include the range of taxes that can contribute most importantly to the 4, now 5, Rs: revenue, redistribution, repricing, representation and reparations. This priority for tax justice is inherently of a different character from the others presented here. Disclosure and enforcement are, arguably, about making tax work so that populations can (justly) choose their preferred outcomes. This priority goes beyond that to support the introduction or strengthening of specific types of tax.

The evidence shows that direct taxes (mainly income taxes on corporates and individuals) tend to be the most salient – that is, the most visible to the public, and therefore can do most to strengthen state–citizen relations of accountability, as well as providing the strongest basis for redistribution. Other specific taxes that tend to be under-utilised, typically because of elite lobbying, include wealth taxes; land value taxes; inheritance taxes; and capital gains taxes. In line with the original, narrower view of 'tax justice' I emphasised, the differential treatment of income from capital and labour remains a major distortion in many systems.

Lastly, there is a clear need for taxes that respond to the climate crisis – but, crucially, only as part of a broader package of inter- and intra-national distribution that ensures the overall effects are progressive and reflect the loss and damage caused predominantly by one group of countries. A key concern is that 'efficiency' arguments for regressive carbon taxes will dominate discussions, creating a false trade-off in which addressing within-country inequalities and between-country inequalities is framed as a competing aim to effective reduction of planetary damage. Efficiency arguments tend to support taxes that are less immediately 'distorting' for corporate investment, for example, even if the result may be less progressive – while redistributive taxes tend to be cast as less efficient, even if as in the case of corporate income tax, economic analysis suggests the reverse is true.

Naïve carbon pricing measures to discourage emissions are almost inevitably regressive. That is, if we simply increase the per unit price of emissions, higher inequality will result. Lower-income households will pay a higher share of their incomes, for a problem to which they contributed less. And the same will hold for lower-income countries, whose responsibility for historic emissions is a fraction of that of the former imperial powers who between them have used up the great majority of the planetary breathing space over the last centuries.

The alternative view would recognise and prioritise two points that are missing from this reductive view. First, the value of protecting the planet is above all in order to promote human well-being. Reducing carbon emissions (or other damage) to a safer level by sacrificing human well-being – at the cost of making life impossibly expensive for the lowest-income groups – would constitute a failure rather than a trade-off. And second, it is short-sighted at best to imagine that growing policy-led inequalities can be ignored while maintaining the political support necessary to achieve sustained improvements in emissions and other planetary damage over decades. That is, if climate policies are understood as punitive for the poorest, and making inequality and social outcomes worse, there is little chance that governments will be elected to pursue them.

Such approaches also fail to recognise the historic responsibility of the richest countries for the damage done (Figure 4.4). Nor does it reflect the entirely disproportionate role of the richest households. As Lucas Chancel (2022, p. 931) finds: 'the bottom 50% of the world population emitted 12% of global emissions in 2019, whereas the top 10% emitted 48% of the total. Since 1990, the bottom 50% of the world population has been responsible for only 16% of all emissions growth, whereas the top 1% has been responsible for 23% of the total. While per-capita emissions of the global top 1% increased since 1990, emissions from low- and middle-income groups within rich countries declined.'

This pattern of responsibility does create, however, an important opportunity to align taxation of planetarily damaging behaviours. The global distribution of income and wealth, and the observed propensities to emit carbon, imply the possibility that progressive taxation of income and wealth can reduce within-country inequalities *and* emissions, *and* also generate revenues to support countries with least responsibility for historic emissions and the greatest vulnerability to climate damage today.

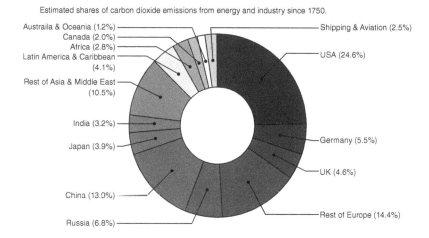

Estimated shares of carbon dioxide emissions from energy and industry since 1750.

Figure 4.4 Cumulative carbon dioxide emissions, 1750–2020

Source: Tietjen (2022). Chart from The Conversation/CC-BY-ND, using data from Our World In Data, Global Carbon Project.

Further work is needed to understand fully the basis for the excess emissions of the richest households, which stems from their investments more than their consumption. But a politically feasible path can be envisaged towards a climate tax justice approach that reflects responsibility and reduces both within-country and between-country inequalities. With comprehensive redistributive measures that ensure the revenues are overwhelmingly targeted to those countries and populations that bear the impacts but not the responsibility for the climate crisis, carbon taxes may have a role to play as part of a reparative effort, rather than a policy approach that deepens historic injustice.

International and institutional measures

The final set of measures to deliver tax justice relate to the international and institutional changes needed, and address the international rules and their control. Collectively, they aim to ensure that anonymous ownership of assets, including control of legal entities, is comprehensively barred; that corporate tax abuses through profit shifting becomes equally impossible; and that the global architecture for setting tax and transparency rules is remade into an inclusive, transparent framework under UN auspices.

Create a global asset registry

A global asset registry, or a GAR, completes a key piece of the puzzle by joining up the previous transparency measures. This proposal, now supported also by the Independent Commission for the Reform of International Corporate Taxation and earlier proposed by two of its commissioners Thomas Piketty and Gabriel Zucman, would see the joining up of national-level registers of ultimate beneficial ownership, coupled with the broadening of coverage (ICRICT, 2019, 2022; Knobel, 2019b).

The GAR would include high-value assets of all types, from property and financial accounts to art works and aircraft, and cover all types of legal vehicles and arrangements, including companies, partnerships, trusts and foundations. Some data would be fully public at the individual level (as, for example, company ownership should be already), while some data (such as bank account ownership) would likely remain private to certain authorities only for enforcement purposes – not only for tax but broader regulation, including of economic sanctions.

The GAR ultimately provides the basis both to facilitate wealth taxes of all types and ensure their effectiveness, and also to allow fully informed political debate and policy choices in respect of the levels of wealth inequality that individual countries are willing to tolerate. As Piketty (2014) noted in his book *Capital in the Twenty-First Century*, these are the two sustained benefits of the land register that was established during the French Revolution – informed public debate around inequalities, and the scope for taxation. Together these can support both greater equality and a stronger democratic engagement on questions of redistribution in general.

An estimated 50% of the wealth held undeclared offshore belongs to the most wealthy 0.01% of households (Alstadsæter et al., 2018). Perhaps a tenth of global household wealth, and a third of multinationals' profits, are held or booked in offshore jurisdictions. It would seem a basic requirement for functional governance that there is minimal transparency and traceability of these assets and income streams, of such scale in relation to the global economy.

The question for policymakers is not 'why would we collect and join up data to create this global public good?', but why wouldn't we? The technical exercise is large but not inordinately complex. The potential benefits are vast: to put a comprehensive end to anonymous ownership and all the tax abuse and other corrupt practices that it supports.

From arm's-length pricing to unitary taxation

When the League of Nations chose separate entity accounting and bound the world to the arm's-length principle for a century, as explained in the previous chapter, the alternative they chose *against* was unitary taxation with formulary apportionment. That is the basis towards which international tax rules must now move, and have finally if slowly begun to do so.

There are technical aspects to this proposal, but at the core is the simplest possible approach. Multinationals make their profits, and their key decisions, at the level of the whole group. They should equally be taxed at that level. Then the question is how to divide the taxable profits between countries, and the answer is to give each country as tax base, the share of profits that corresponds to the share of the multinational's economic activity that each country hosts.

Unitary taxation rests on the idea of assessing a multinational's profits at the level of the group, as a single unit, rather than at the level of the separate entities that make up the group. Rather than worry about the construction of artificial and easily manipulated transfer prices for intra-group transactions, the key question becomes how to allocate between countries the globally assessed profits of the group as a whole.

The answer is to apply a formula, allocating the global profits according to the location of the multinational's real activity. For example, if 10% of a multinational's sales take place in the UK, and 10% of its employment also, then 10% of the global profits should be allocated to the UK for taxation at the standard rate of corporate income tax.

This process – known as formulary apportionment – is in widespread use for the allocation of taxable profit within *subnational* jurisdictions. This includes all the states of the US; the provinces of Canada; and the cantons of Switzerland (Picciotto, 2012, 2017). That is, a major company operating across a range of different US states will see a share of its US profit apportioned to each US state for them to levy tax on. Various formulae are in use. Some US states combine sales, employment and assets; others use single factors only, most commonly sales. Canadian provinces use a common formula, combining sales and employment.

It is only in the last decade that the potential to establish unitary taxation internationally has become a realistic possibility again. As researchers have noted, the availability of country-by-country reporting data has significantly strengthened the case for unitary taxation, by providing a continuing stream of evidence on the extent and nature of profit 'mis-alignment' (Viegas & Dias, 2021) – which is perhaps the reason why the professional enablers of tax abuse have fought so hard to resist it becoming public.

Recall the single goal that the G20 group of countries gave the OECD, back in 2013: to achieve a better alignment of taxable profits with the location of multinationals' real economic activity. But the first BEPS (Base Erosion and Profit Shifting) process was constrained to retain the arm's-length principle, making substantial progress almost impossible.

The second BEPS process that began in January 2019 did so from a starting point of consensus that the arm's-length principle was no longer fit for purpose and could not deliver on the G20's goal. Two pillars were proposed: Pillar One would allocate profit differently (going 'beyond arm's-length pricing'), and Pillar Two would ensure a minimum tax rate for all profits.

The most ambitious proposal for Pillar One came from the G-24 inter-governmental group of countries and called for apportionment of all profits. Proposals from OECD members like the UK and US were much more limited, seeking to apply unitary approaches only to certain 'digital' and related sectors. In the end, the ambition collapsed almost entirely. The latest proposals (as at August 2023) would see a sales-only formula applied to a small fraction only of the profits of less than a hundred multinationals. All other profits of these and all other multinationals would remain as before – despite the starting point for the process being that the arm's-length principle is not fit for purpose. On top of this, the proposal is constructed so that the OECD's biggest member, the United States, is able to block implementation for every country singlehandedly – and the US Congress looks certain to do so.

The State of Tax Justice reports (Tax Justice Network, e.g. 2021, 2023) take what is effectively a formulary approach to assess the degree of profit misalignment. That is, they compare the current distribution of profit and real economic activity, to see how far profit shifting results in a divergence from what a unitary approach with formulary apportionment would gener-ate. The findings on the scale of corporate tax abuse can therefore equally be interpreted as the potential gains from introducing a formulary approach.

The direct, global gain in annual revenue stands at $311 billion. The absolute gains are largest for the major economies, including the UK. The most intense gains, in terms of current tax revenues and public spend-ing, accrue to lower-income countries. Taxing in this way would also strengthen genuine market competition. At present, multinationals enjoy an effective subsidy due to their tax abuse, when compared to standalone domestic businesses which by definition pay their taxes in the location of their real economic activity.

Pillar Two remains alive, and a minimum tax rate of 15% is likely to be introduced by EU countries and some others. But the approach is undermined by the absence of measures to stop profit shifting, and the introduction of complex carveouts that will allow a real rate of nearer 10% to be considered compliant. Latest analysis shows that the main beneficiaries are likely to be profit shifting conduit jurisdictions, while others gain little or nothing (Reitz, 2023) – although the norm-setting power of introducing a minimum tax should not be dismissed.

With the OECD proposals having lost most of their ambition, and offering little if any new revenues for lower-income countries (BEPS Monitoring Group, 2023; Picciotto et al., 2023), governments are once again looking to unilateral alternatives. Under discussion are broader apportionment methods including the 2019 proposal of the G-24 group of countries discussed in the previous chapter. A turning point may have been reached. The unitary tax approach long championed by the tax justice movement has shifted from being unthinkable, to being part of international negotiations, and increasingly now appearing as a realistic end-point. Whether that can be achieved through the OECD is another question, and increasingly such a discussion – that would directly address global inequalities in taxing rights – is seen as a possibility within the mooted UN framework for international tax cooperation.

Global governance: Replace the rich countries' club

In 1999 former director of fiscal affairs at the IMF, Vito Tanzi, proposed that the prime function of an international tax organisation should be to 'make tax systems consistent with the public interest of the whole world rather than the public interest of specific countries'. One organisation that has attempted to remedy the situation is the OECD, which has a considerable expertise in this area, but this poses problems because the OECD only represents the rich nations of the world and many nations are consequently excluded from its decision-making process. The most appropriate body to take on the functions... would be the United Nations.

Tax Justice Network (2005a)

The overarching challenge for tax justice today, as it was when the Tax Justice Network was launched, is to establish a globally inclusive framework for tax cooperation. Global governance of tax in the 21st century requires a genuinely inclusive and representative forum at the UN to replace the rich country members' club, the OECD.

The G77 group of 134 lower-income countries has consistently proposed an intergovernmental tax body under UN auspices, and while there remains fierce resistance from some OECD countries to giving up their current disproportionate power, disillusionment with the OECD process has now created the possibility of a broader coalition.

A breakthrough in the 2022 UN General Assembly saw a resolution unanimously adopted, mandating the Secretary-General to prepare a report on the options and modalities for negotiating such a framework, and beginning intergovernmental discussion. The resolution was tabled by the Africa Group, following the ECA finance ministers' May 2022 declaration in favour of a UN tax convention, and continuing the region's global leadership on these issues.

A UN framework convention on tax could play multiple roles in delivering tax justice. It could set inclusively negotiated minimum standards for transparency. In effect, it could ensure that the full benefits of the ABC of tax transparency are delivered to all countries and peoples, while creating a global asset registry as a public good. Above all, the convention could create the forum under UN auspices for the transparent and globally inclusive negotiation of future tax rules and standards, including unitary taxation.

A draft convention text published by Eurodad and the Global Alliance for Tax Justice provides a clear sense of the possibilities across all of these areas (Ryding, 2022; see also the proposals of Chowdhary & Picciotto, 2021, and Quiñones, 2023; and, of course, Tanzi, 1999). Embedding this breadth and ambition within a convention designed as a human rights instrument could ensure that the technical and political bases of the measure are jointly maintained and mutually reinforcing.

Of all the international measures for tax justice, this reshaping of the global architecture is the most badly needed and potentially transformativo.

It can make possible directly the international and transparency elements set out here, and at the same time remove the full set of international obstacles to domestic measures.

The Secretary-General's report identifies a framework convention as the central option, which could include specific protocols to address particular issues, as well as create the governance structure for future negotiations over tax rules. The protocols could be used to create the fully multilateral, automatic exchange of information that the OECD has so far failed to deliver, and to set international standards for public registers of beneficial ownership information and public country-by-country reporting by multinationals. They could go further in beneficial ownership transparency and lay the grounds for a global asset registry.

The negotiation of international tax rules would allow for coordination of an emerging shift towards unitary taxation; and across the piece, the entire process would take place within the broadly transparent, and deliberately democratic decision-making structures of the United Nations. Where OECD decisions are taken by 'consensus' (you are deemed to agree unless you raise a specific objection), and privately (so that it can never be known whether governments' negotiating positions reflected their public statements), the UN offers openness of both negotiations and voting patterns. The potential for public accountability, including as an anecdote to the private lobbying of tax abusers and their professional enablers, has a powerful appeal.

conclusion

The tax justice movement has been successful in bringing a range of specific tools and approaches onto the policy agenda for both national and international decisions. But much more important has been the raising of public awareness, in countries all around the world, about the importance and the potential of tax issues for all of our lives. And there is much more to do!

The UN Millennium Development Goals (MDGs) ran from 2000 to 2015. Together, the eight MDGs made up the first global framework for policies designed to drive forward progress in countries with lower per capita incomes. Extraordinary as it now seems, the MDGs did not even refer to tax.

The MDGs' successor framework reflects a complete about-turn. The Sustainable Development Goals (SDGs), which run from 2015 to 2030, identify tax as the *primary* means of implementation. Target 17.1 requires member states to 'strengthen domestic resource mobilisation, including through international support'. It is the key element in the toolkit to achieve the first 16 targets which range from curbing inequalities to obtaining sharp reductions in childhood mortality.

Within those, SDG 16.4 represents a major victory for African leadership. This collective global target to curb illicit financial flows results directly from the work of the High Level Panel on Illicit Financial Flows out of Africa, chaired by former South African president Thabo Mbeki.

Their 2015 report achieved the unanimous backing of African Union members, and established the issue of illicit financial flows as a major priority for the region and globally. The underlying definitions matter too, because the panel had demonstrated that illicit flows are dominated by cross-border tax abuse – and above all, by corporate tax abuse committed by multinationals from OECD countries. That analysis eventually prevailed in the formal statistical definition adopted by the UN, despite heavy lobby from OECD countries to exclude corporate tax entirely.

And so, the SDGs show a quite different view of the world from the MDGs. The first framework focused on the role of aid from high-income countries in supporting development efforts for lower-income countries. The successor recognises that national tax, not aid, is and must be the central source of funds for any country. And more than that, it targets illicit financial flows, and calls for international support (in effect, from the OECD countries primarily responsible), not in the form of further aid but through cooperation to curb the abuse.

The High Level Panel's success here, and the longstanding support of the G77 group, also lies behind the UN resolution adopted in late 2022 which has triggered intergovernmental discussions on a UN tax framework.

Forcing open the necessary political space over the course of two decades has been a burgeoning tax justice movement. This has been powered by a combination of strategic movement-building and swift reaction to opportunities – not least, the financial crisis that began in 2008, and the crucial work of investigative journalists including the ICIJ in exposing specific, high-profile cases.

Leading international development NGOs like Christian Aid and ActionAid played an important role in building public awareness, in the global North, of the impact of tax abuse on lower-income countries. When the crisis struck, and fiscal pressures took on a different complexion at home, there was a base of public awareness due to this work and the growing media profile of tax abuse. In addition, the development NGOs, now including Oxfam and others too, had begun to exert significant political influence on policymakers in the aid donor countries of the global North.

The financial crisis triggered a wave of public anger. This reflected public recognition of the dangers of financial deregulation, and a growing sense during public spending cuts that major companies and wealthy individuals were not paying their share of taxes (Vaughan, 2019).

As former US president Ronald Reagan was fond of saying, politicians don't see the light – they feel the heat. Over two decades, politicians in countries like the UK have become progressively more aware of public anger and demands over tax abuse in particular. This contributed significantly to the willingness to take on elements of the tax justice agenda at the G8 and G20 groups of countries, and at the OECD.

The progress that has been made at the OECD, however, remains piecemeal at the very best. Previous chapters have surveyed evidence of the continuing growth in the share of global GDP which multinationals claim as profit, and evidence of the simultaneous failure even to maintain a proportionate share for the tax revenues of countries around the world. Evidence of how offshore tax abuse has continued to thrive. Of how the professional enablers and secrecy jurisdictions seem consistently to react to exposure by claiming that the leaks are old news, and they've cleaned up their act. Until the next time...

The Global Alliance for Tax Justice, as an umbrella group for mass mobilisation organisations all around the world, has played a critical role in maintaining both heat and light on these issues. Its support, along with the Civil Society Group on Financing for Development, has contributed significantly to the engagement of key actors within the United Nations. The engagement of investor groups on key questions, and of the labour movement including through the global union federation Public Services International, has brought important additional momentum and access to policymakers. A critical shift has been the engagement of the tax justice and human rights movements, including with partners like the Centre for Economic and Social Rights, and the emergence of a powerful narrative around the centrality of tax justice for women's rights and for human rights more broadly.

If there is a missing section in the last chapter, it would be one dedicated not to policy areas but to the demand that people MOBILISE! The heat on policymakers is generated only when sufficient members of the public get involved, through civil society organisations and through more and less direct channels of political engagement. If you want change, you have to raise the temperature. That starts with demanding better, nationally, for our societies. Recognising the linkages means that we need to mobilise for international action too.

And the direction of travel for tax justice over the coming years is closely bound with the success of the UN intergovernmental discussions, and the scope to move into formal negotiations over a UN tax convention and global tax body. Such a convention, as set out above, has the potential to deliver progress right across the multiple, technical elements in the tax justice agenda. Table 5.1 covers the core elements of the agenda, the A to G[3] of tax justice. The ABC of tax transparency, *and* the international and institutional elements, could be met through a convention. Delivering on these would also bolster the scope for, and benefits of, both disclosure and enforcement at the national level, and strengthen the hand of those pursuing better taxation more generally.

Table 5.1 The ABCDEFG[3] of tax justice

	Transparency	Domestic	International & institutional
A	Automatic information exchange		
B	Beneficial ownership transparency		
C	Country-by-country reporting		
D		Disclosure	
E		Enforcement	
F			Formulary apportionment and unitary taxation
G		Good taxes	
G(2)			Global asset registry
G(3)			Global governance reform

Most importantly, a UN tax convention could respond to the fundamentally *political* nature of tax. It could ensure that there is, finally, a globally inclusive, political forum to take decisions on issues which are key both to the inequalities *between* countries, and the ability of people *within* countries to set their own path and curb the overlapping inequalities they themselves face.

Opening up the global governance of tax rules and transparency has the potential to deliver significant benefits for everyone – everyone except the tax abusers and their professional enablers. As for the small number of jurisdictions, including the UK, that facilitate the majority of abuse at others' expense: our societies too stand to benefit, by reducing our over-reliance on a corrupting growth of the financial sector, and the inequalities and democratic damage that brings with it.

The issues discussed in this short book may be technical in part, but they are political in their entirety. The visibility that we have about our taxes; the accountability that we demand in exchange; and the choices that we make: these are *our* choices to make. We make them within the constraints of the international rules and institutions that set them. But these institutions too are the result of our choices and actions, or the absence of actions.

Tax can play a valuable role in helping us to organise ourselves to live good lives while managing the climate crisis. And just as tax has played a major part in each of the three imperial ages of illicit financial flows outlined above, tax can make a contribution to reparative justice too.

The tax justice agenda has the potential to deliver benefits to the great majority of people in every part of the world – by bolstering all of our freedom to choose how we organise ourselves as societies, to live better lives together.

Tax is our social superpower. We must demand that it be deployed for us all.

references

ACIJ, CELS, Dejusticia, FUNDAR, INESC, Red de Justicia Fiscal de América Latina y El Caribe & CESR, 2021, *Principles for Human Rights in Fiscal Policy*, New York: Center for Economic and Social Rights, https://www.cesr.org/sites/default/files/2021/Principles_for_Human_Rights_in_Fiscal_Policy-ENG-VF-1.pdf (accessed 12.8.2023).

ActionAid, 2012 (2010), *Calling Time: Why SABMiller Should Stop Dodging Taxes in Africa*, London: ActionAid, https://web.archive.org/web/20130123193521/http://www.actionaid.org.uk:80/doc_lib/calling_time_on_tax_avoidance.pdf (accessed 28.3.2023).

Adam, C., & Bevan, D., 2004, 'Fiscal policy design in low-income countries' in T. Addison & A. Roe (eds.), *Fiscal Policy for Development*, Basingstoke: Palgrave Macmillan/UNU-WIDER.

Adam, S., Delestre, I., & Nair, V., 2022, 'Corporation tax and investment', ch. 6 in IFS, *Green Budget 2022*, https://ifs.org.uk/publications/corporation-tax-and-investment (accessed 12.8.2023).

Adeyeye, B., & Otusanya, J., 2015, 'The impact of taxpayers' perception of government's accountability, transparency and reduction in fiscal corruption on voluntary tax compliance in Nigeria', *International Journal of Economics and Accounting* 6(3), 276–299.

Advani, A., Elming, W., & Shaw, J., 2023, 'The dynamic effects of tax audits', *Review of Economics and Statistics*, https://doi.org/10.1162/rest_a_01101 (accessed 28.3.2023).

Afrobarometer, 2023, 'Accountability is gaining ground', *The Continent* 121 (25 March).

Agyemang, E., 2023, 'OECD pressed Australia over plan to reveal where multinationals pay tax', *Financial Times*, 7 July, https://www.ft.com/content/b21cfde0-8940-45db-b3e3-3e9807d7b957 (accessed 12.8.2023).

Ahrens, L., Hakelberg, L., & Rixen, T., 2022, 'A victim of regulatory arbitrage? Automatic exchange of information and the use of golden visas and corporate shells', *Regulation and Governance* 16(3), 653–672, https://doi.org/10.1111/rego.12363.

Allingham, M., & Sandmo, A., 1972, 'Income tax evasion: a theoretical analysis', *Journal of Public Economics* 1(3-4), 323–338.

Alm, J., 2019, 'What motivates tax compliance?', *Journal of Economic Surveys* 33(2), 353–388.

Alm, J., McClelland, G., & Schulze, W., 1992, 'Why do people pay taxes?', *Journal of Public Economics* 48(1), 21–38.

Al-Maghrebi, M., Sapiei, N., & Abdullah, M., 2022, 'Power, trust and transparency as determinant factors of tax compliance: A systematic review', *Journal of Tax Reform* 8(3), 312–335.

Alstadsæter, A., Johannesen, N., & Zucman, G., 2018, 'Who owns the wealth in tax havens? Macro evidence and implications for global inequality', *Journal of Public Economics* 162, 89–100.

Alstadsæter, A., Johannesen, N. & Zucman, G., 2019, 'Tax evasion and inequality', *American Economic Review* 109(6), 2073–2103.

Aliu, F., Redonda, A., & von Haldewang, C., 2022, 'The Global Tax Expenditure Database (GTED) Progress Report', *GTED* (13 April), https://gted.net/2022/04/the-global-tax-expenditures-database-gted-progress-report/ (accessed 28.3.2023).

Ates, L., Cobham, A., Harari, M., Janský, P., Meinzer, M., Millan-Narotzky, L., & Palanský, M., 2021, 'The corporate tax haven index: A new geography of profit shifting', in B. Unger, L. Russel, & J. Ferwerda (eds.), *Combatting Fiscal Fraud and Empowering Regulators*, Oxford: Oxford University Press.

AU/ECA, 2015, *Illicit Financial Flows: Report of the High Level Panel on Illicit Financial Flows from Africa*, Addis Ababa: Economic Commission for Africa.

Bachas, P., Fisher-Post, M., Jensen, A., & Zucman, G.,'2023, 'Globalization and factor income taxation', NBER working paper 29819: https://globaltaxation.world/ (accessed 4 August 2023).

BBC, 2023, 'UK pays EU £1.7bn to settle long-running import fraud case', 10 February, https://www.bbc.com/news/uk-politics-64587483 (accessed 12.8.2023).

BEPS Monitoring Group, 2023, 'Taxing multinationals: The BEPS proposals and alternatives', *BEPS Monitoring Briefing*, 5 July, https://www.bepsmonitoringgroup.org/news/2023/7/5/the-beps-proposals-and-alternatives (accessed 12.8.2023).

Berkowitz, D., Richard, J.-F., & Pistor, K., 2003, 'Economic development, legality, and the transplant effect', *European Economic Review* 47(1), 165–195.

Bhambra, G.., 2022, 'Imperial revenue and national welfare: The case of Britain' in G. K. Bhambra, & J. McClure (eds.), *Imperial Inequalities*, Manchester: Manchester University Press.

Bhambra, G., & McClure, J. (eds.), 2022, *Imperial Inequalities*, Manchester: Manchester University Press.

Bilicka, K., 2019, 'Comparing UK tax returns of foreign multinationals to matched domestic firms', *American Economic Review* 109(8), 2921–2953.

Bilicka, K., 2022, 'Why are the contributions of multinational firms to corporate tax revenue declining?', *Oxford Bulletin of Economics and Statistics* 84(2), 401–426.

Black, T., Bloomquist, K., Emblom, E., Johns, A., Plumley, A., & Stuk, E., 2012, 'Federal tax compliance research: Tax year 2006 tax gap estimation', *IRS Research, Analysis & Statistics Working Paper*.

Boland-Rudder, H., 2015, 'HSBC pays Swiss authorities record-breaking fine', *ICIJ.org* (4 June), https://www.icij.org/inside-icij/2015/06/hsbc-pays-swiss-authorities-record-breaking-fine/.

Boyce, J., & Ndikumana, L., 2000, 'Is Africa a net creditor? New estimates of capital flight from severely indebted African countries, 1970–1996', *PERI Working Paper* 5.

Bracco, E., Porcelli, F., & Redoano, M., 2019, 'Political competition, tax salience and accountability. Theory and evidence from Italy', *European Journal of Political Economy* 58, 138–163.

Brooks, C., Godfrey, C., Hillenbrand, C., & Money, K., 2016, 'Do investors care about corporate taxes?', *Journal of Corporate Finance* 38, 218–248.

Brown, D., 2021, *The Whiteness of Wealth: How the Tax System Impoverishes Black Americans and How We Can Fix It*, New York: Crown.

Brown, D., 2023, 'The Gullah Geechee fight for a legacy after slavery', *The Guardian* (30 March), https://www.theguardian.com/news/ng-interactive/2023/mar/30/white-gold-from-black-hands-the-gullah-geechee-fight-for-a-legacy-after-slavery-manchester (accessed 30.3.2023).

Bullough, O., 2019, 'How Britain can help you get away with stealing millions: A five-step guide', *The Guardian* (5 July), https://www.theguardian.com/world/2019/jul/05/how-britain-can-help-you-get-away-with-stealing-millions-a-five-step-guide (accessed 28.3.2023).

Carter, P., & Cobham, A., 2016, 'Are taxes good for your health?', *UNU-WIDER Working Paper* 171.

Casi, E., Spengel, C., & Stage, B., 2020, 'Cross-border tax evasion after the common reporting standard: Game over?', *Journal of Public Economics* 190, 104240.

CBO, 2020, 'Trends in the Internal Revenue Service's funding and enforcement', *CBO.gov* (July), https://www.cbo.gov/publication/56467 (accessed 28.3.2023).

Chancel, L., 2022, 'Global carbon inequality over 1990–2019', *Nature Sustainability* 5, 931–938.

Chowdhary, A., & Picciotto, S., 2021, 'Streamlining the architecture of international tax through a UN framework convention on tax cooperation', *South Centre Tax Cooperation Policy Brief* 21, https://www.southcentre.int/tax-cooperation-policy-brief-21-november-2021/ (accessed 28.3.2023).

Christensen, J., 2012, 'Happy Birthday Tax Justice Network', *TJN blog* (9 November), https://taxjustice.blogspot.com/2012/11/happy-birthday-tax-justice-network.html (accessed 28.3.2023).

Christensen, J., Shaxson, N., & Wigan, D., 2016, 'The finance curse: Britain and the world economy', *British Journal of Politics and International Relations* 18(1), 255–269.

Christensen, R., 2021, 'Elite professionals in transnational tax governance', *Global Networks* 21(2), 265–293.

Christensen, R., Seabrooke, L., & Wigan, D. 2022, 'Professional action in global wealth chains', *Regulation and Governance* 16(3), 705–721.

Cobham, A., 2005, 'Taxation policy and development', *OCGG Economy Analysis* 2, Oxford Council on Good Governance: https://bit.ly/tax4Rs.

Cobham, A., 2007, 'The tax consensus has failed!', *Oxford Council on Good Governance Economy Section Recommendation* 8: http://taxjustice.net/cms/upload/pdf/Cobham_Tax_Consensus_Failed_08.pdf (accessed 28.3.2023).

Cobham, A., 2014, 'Has the US U-turned on tax information exchange?', *Center for Global Development* (6 November), https://www.cgdev.org/blog/has-united-states-u-turned-tax-information-exchange (accessed 28.3.2023).

Cobham, A., 2016, 'Corporate tax in the UK: The triumph of "austerity" over evidence', *Austerity and its Alternatives research paper (McMaster University)*, https://facsocsci.mcmaster.ca/austerity-and-its-alternatives/documents/w14-oct-3-2017-alex-cobham-corporate-tax-in-the-uk.pdf (accessed 12.8.2023).

Cobham, A., 2019, *The Uncounted*, Cambridge: Polity Press.

Cobham, A., 2020, 'Investors demand OECD tax transparency', *Tax Justice Network* (19 March), https://taxjustice.net/2020/03/19/investors-demand-oecd-tax-transparency/ (accessed 28.3.2023).

Cobham, A., 2022, 'Imperial extraction and "tax havens"', in G. Bhambra & J. McClure (eds.), *Imperial Inequalities*, Manchester: Manchester University Press.

Cobham, A., Etter-Phoya, R., Meinzer, M., Abugre, C., Monkam, N., Lépissier, A., & Mosioma, A., 2019, 'Vulnerability and exposure to illicit financial flows risk in Africa', London: Tax Justice Network/ African Tax Administration forum/ COFFERS Combating Fiscal Fraud and Empowering Regulators/Tax Justice Network Africa, https://taxjustice.net/reports/vulnerability-and-exposure-to-illicit-financial-flows-risk-in-africa/.

Cobham, A., Garcia-Bernardo, J., Harari, M., Lépissier, A., Lima, S., Meinzer, M., Montoya, L., & Moreno, L., 2021, 'Vulnerability and exposure to illicit financial flows risk in Latin America', Tax Justice Network/Latindadd, https://taxjustice. net/reports/vulnerability-and-exposure-to-illicit-financial-flows-risk-in-latin-america/.

Cobham, A., Gray, J., & Murphy, R., 2017, 'What do they pay? Towards a public database to account for the economic activities and tax contributions of multinational corporations', *Open Data for Tax Justice white paper*, https:// datafortaxjustice.net/what-do-they-pay/ (accessed 28.3.2023).

Cobham, A., & Janský, P., 2018, 'Global distribution of revenue loss from corporate tax avoidance: Re-estimation and country results', *Journal of International Development* 30/2, 206–232.

Cobham, A., & Janský, P., 2019, 'Measuring misalignment: The location of US multinationals' economic activity versus the location of their profits', *Development Policy Review* 37(1), 91–110.

Cobham, A., & Janský, P., 2020, *Estimating Illicit Financial Flows: A Critical Guide to the Data, Methodologies, and Findings*, Oxford: Oxford University Press.

Cobham, A., Janský, P., & Meinzer, M., 2015, 'The financial secrecy index: Shedding new light on the geography of secrecy', *Economic Geography* 91(3), 281–303.

Cobham, A., Janský, P., & Meinzer, M., 2018, 'A half-century of resistance to corporate disclosure', *Transnational Corporations Journal* 25(3), https:// unctad.org/system/files/official-document/diaeia2018d5a2_en.pdf (accessed 28.3.2023).

Conne, J., 2010, 'HSBC: Chinese for making money', *Le Monde Diplomatique* (February), https://mondediplo.com/2010/02/04hsbc.

Credit Suisse, 2022, 'Credit Suisse responds', *OCCRP.org*, https://www.occrp. org/en/suisse-secrets/credit-suisse-responds.

Crivelli, E., de Mooij, R., & Keen, M., 2016, 'Base erosion, profit shifting and developing countries', *FinanzArchiv: Public Finance Analysis* 72/3, 268–301.

CTJ, 1996, Citizens for Tax Justice website, https://web.archive.org/ web/19961101191653/http://www.ctj.org/ (accessed 15/9/2022).

Davis, M., 2000, *Late Victorian Holocausts: El Niño Famines and the Making of the Third World*, London: Verso.

Decolonising Economics in coordination with Tax Justice UK and Tax Justice Network, 2022, *Tax as a tool for racial justice*, https://decolonisingeconomics. org/2022/09/09/tax-as-a-tool-for-racial-justice-report/ (accessed 28.2.2023).

Devereux, M., 2021, 'What will the Budget do for corporate investment?', *Oxford University Centre for Business Taxation* (5 March), https://oxfordtax.sbs.

ox.ac.uk/article/what-will-the-budget-do-for-corporate-investment (accessed 12.8.2023).

Devereux, M., Freedman, J., & Vella, J., 2012, *Tax Avoidance*, https://dx.doi.org/10.2139/ssrn.3754562.

Dihmis, L., 2021, ''LuxLetters' investigation uncovers tax loophole in Luxembourg', *OCCRP.org*, https://www.occrp.org/en/daily/14769-luxletters-investigation-uncovers-tax-loophole-in-luxembourg (accessed 28.3.2023).

Drucker, J., & Hakim, D., 2021, 'How accounting giants craft favorable tax rules from inside government', *New York Times*, 19 September, https://www.nytimes.com/2021/09/19/business/accounting-firms-tax-loopholes-government.html (accessed 12.8.2023).

Eberhartinger, E., Speitmann, R., & Sureth-Sloane, C., 2020, 'Real effects of public country-by-country reporting and the firm structure of European banks', *WU International Taxation Research Paper 2020–01.*

ECORYS, 2021, *Monitoring the Amount of Wealth Hidden by Individuals in International Financial Centres and Impact of Recent Internationally Agreed Standards on Tax Transparency on the Fight against Tax Evasion*, Brussels: European Commission DG TAXUD.

Elzayn, H., Smith, E., Hertz, T., Ramesh, A., Fisher, R., Ho, D., & Goldin, J., 2023, 'Measuring and mitigating racial disparities in tax audits', *Stanford Institute for Economic Policy Research* Working Paper: https://siepr.stanford.edu/publications/measuring-and-mitigating-racial-disparities-tax-audits/ (accessed 12.8.2023).

Fairness Foundation, 2023, 'Britons want a bigger role for the state in delivering a social contract' (31 March), https://fairnessfoundation.com/role-of-gov (accessed 7.8.2023).

Fastenrath, F., Marx, P., Truger, A., & Vitt, H., 2022, 'Why is it so difficult to tax the rich? Evidence from German policy-makers', *Journal of European Public Policy* 29(5), 767–786.

FATF, 2023, *Guidance on Beneficial Ownership for Legal Persons*, Paris: Financial Action Task Force, http://www.fatf-gafi.org/publications/FATFrecommendations/guidance-beneficial-ownership-legalpersons.html (accessed 28.3.2023).

Fennell, S., 2017, 'Vorlesung international law and the economy in a postcolonial world: Colonialism, institutions and development' [online video, 14 November], available at: https://timms.uni-tuebingen.de:443/tp/UT_20171114_001_intlaw_0001 (accessed 28.3.2023).

Filippin, A., Fiorio, C., & Viviano, E., 2013, 'The effect of tax enforcement on tax morale', *European Journal of Political Economy* 32, 320–331.

FitzGerald, V., & Cobham, A., 2000, 'Capital flight: Causes, effects, magnitude and implications for development', *DFID Background Paper*, London: Department for International Development.

Freedman, J., 2004, 'Defining taxpayer responsibility: In support of a general anti-avoidance principle', *British Tax Review* 4, 332–357.

Frey, B. & Torgler, B.,'2007, 'Tax morale and conditional cooperation', *Journal of Comparative Economics* 35(1), 136–159.

Fulton, L., 2020, *The impact of austerity on tax collection*, Brussels: EPSU, https://www.epsu.org/sites/default/files/article/files/EPSU%20Report%20 Impact_austerity_tax_EN.pdf (accessed 28.3.2023).

GAO, 2022, 'Internal Revenue Service: Information about funding, financial reporting controls, and GAO recommendations', *GAO.gov* (28 November), https://www.gao.gov/assets/gao-23-106351.pdf (accessed 28.3.2023).

Garcia-Bernardo, J., & Janský, P., 2023, 'Profit shifting of multinational companies worldwide', *SSRN working paper*: https://dx.doi.org/10.2139/ssrn.4435224 (accessed 11.8.2023).

Garcia-Bernardo, J., Janský, P., & Tørsløv, T., 2021, 'Multinational corporations and tax havens: Evidence from country-by-country reporting', *International Tax and Public Finance* 28, 1519–1561.

Gechert, S., & Heimberger, P., 2022, 'Do corporate tax cuts boost economic growth?', *European Economic Review* 147, 104157.

Global Forum on Transparency and Exchange of Information for Tax Purposes, 2022, 'Raising the bar on tax transparency', *Global Forum Annual Report 2022*, https://www.oecd.org/tax/transparency/documents/global-forum-annual-report-2022.pdf (accessed 28.3.2023).

GRAIN, 2020, *Digital Fences: The financial enclosure of farmlands in South America*, *GRAIN.org* (September) https://grain.org/en/article/6529-digital-fences-the-financial-enclosure-of-farmlands-in-south-america (accessed 28.3.2023).

GRAIN, 2022, 'The digitalisation of land: more data, less land', *GRAIN.org* (April), https://grain.org/en/article/6832-the-digitalisation-of-land-more-data-less-land (accessed 28.3.2023).

GTED, 2023, 'United Kingdom country profile', https://gted.net/country-profile/ united-kingdom/ (accessed 28.3.2023).

Guyton, J., Langetieg, P., Reck, D., Risch, M., & Zucman, G., 2021, 'Tax evasion at the top of the income distribution: Theory and evidence', *NBER Working Paper* 28542.

Hakelberg, L., 2020, *The Hypocritical Hegemon: How the United States Shapes Global Rules against Tax Evasion and Avoidance*, Ithaca, NY: Cornell University Press.

Hall, S., Illian, J., Makuta, I., McNabb, K., Murray, S., O'Hare, B., Python, A., Zaidi, S., & Bar-Zeev, N., 2021, 'Government revenue and child and maternal mortality', *Open Economies Review* 32, 213–229.

Hall, S., & O'Hare, B., 2022, 'A model to explain the impact of government revenue on the quality of governance and the SDGs', *UNU-WIDER Working Paper* 102, https://www.wider.unu.edu/sites/default/files/Publications/Working-paper/PDF/wp2022-102-model-explain-impact-government-revenue-quality-governance-SDGs.pdf (accessed 28.3.2023).

Ham, C., 2023, *The Rise and Decline of the NHS in England 2000–20: How Political Failure Led to the Crisis in the NHS and Social Care*, London: The King's Fund.

Hamilton, M., 2017, 'HSBC to pay $352m to settle tax evasion charges in finance', *ICIJ.org* (15 November), https://www.icij.org/investigations/swiss-leaks/hsbc-swiss-france-352m-settlement/.

Harker, R., 2019, 'NHS funding and expenditure', *House of Commons Library briefing paper* CBP0724.

He, X., Zhai, F., & Ma, J., 2022, 'The global impact of a carbon border adjustment mechanism: A quantitative assessment', *Task Force on Climate, Development and the IMF*, https://www.bu.edu/gdp/flles/2022/03/TF-WP-001-ГIN.pdf (accessed 12.8.2023).

Heady, C. 2004, 'Taxation policy in low-income countries'; in T. Addison & A. Roe (eds.), *Fiscal Policy for Development*, Basingstoke: Palgrave Macmillan/UNU-WIDER.

Health Foundation, 2022, *Public Perceptions of Health and Social Care: What the New Government Should Know*, London: Health Foundation, https://doi.org/10.37829/HF-2022-P11.

Heimberger, P., & Gechert, S., 2021, 'Corporate tax cuts do not boost growth', *Social Europe* 15 July, https://www.socialeurope.eu/corporate-tax-cuts-do-not-boost-growth (accessed 12.8.2023).

Henry, J., 2012, *The Price of Offshore Revisited: New Estimates for Missing Global Private Wealth, Income, Inequality and Lost Taxes*, London: Tax Justice Network, www.taxjustice.net/cms/upload/pdf/Price_of_Offshore_Revisited_26072012.pdf (accessed 28.3.23).

HMG, 2000, 'Eliminating world poverty: Making globalisation work for the poor', *White Paper on International Development*, London: Her Majesty's Government.

HMRC, 2023, *Measuring Tax Gaps 2023 Edition: Tax Gap Estimates for 2021 to 2022*, London: HM Revenue and Customs, https://www.gov.uk/government/statistics/measuring-tax-gaps (accessed 12.8.2023).

Hobbes, T., 1651, *Leviathan, or, The Matter, Forme, & Power of a Common-wealth Ecclesiasticall and Civil*, https://en.wikisource.org/wiki/Leviathan (accessed 12.8.2023).

House of Commons Committee of Public Accounts, 2013, 'Tax avoidance: The role of large accountancy firms', *Forty-fourth Report of Session 2012–13* HC 870, London: Stationery Office Limited, https://publications.parliament.uk/pa/cm201213/cmselect/cmpubacc/870/870.pdf (accessed 12.8.2023).

HSBC, 2023, 'Purpose, values and strategy', https://www.hsbc.com/who-we-are/purpose-values-and-strategy (accessed 27.3.2023).

Hunady, J., & Orviska, M., 2014, 'Determinants of foreign direct investment in EU countries – Do corporate taxes really matter?', *Procedia Economics and Finance* 12, 243–250.

Hussain, A., & Davies, M., 2022, '"Burner" firms are infiltrating innocent people's houses', *Sunday Times* (27 November), https://www.thetimes.co.uk/article/burner-firms-are-infiltrating-innocent-peoples-houses-h5k5dm2sp (accessed 28.3.2023).

IATF (Inter-Agency Task Force on Financing for Development), 2022, 'Bridging the finance divide', *UN Financing for Sustainable Development Report* 2022 (Table III.A.3, p.48), https://developmentfinance.un.org/fsdr2022 (accessed 28.3.2023).

IBE, 2022, *Attitudes of the British Public to Business Ethics 2022*, London: Institute of Business Ethics, https://www.ibe.org.uk/resource/publicattitudes2022.html (accessed 28.3.2023).

ICIJ, 2017, 'Explore the Panama Papers key figures', *ICIJ.org*, https://www.icij.org/investigations/panama-papers/explore-panama-papers-key-figures/.

ICIJ, 2021, 'Paradise Papers: Secrets of the global elite', *ICIJ.org* https://www.icij.org/investigations/paradise-papers/ (accessed 28.3.2023).

ICIJ, 2023, 'Swiss Leaks', https://www.icij.org/investigations/swiss-leaks/explore-swiss-leaks-data/ (accessed 27.3.2023).

ICRICT, 2019, 'A roadmap for a global asset registry: Measuring and tackling inequality: Curbing tax avoidance, tax evasion, corruption and illicit financial flows', *ICRICT*, https://www.icrict.com/press-release/2019/3/25/icrictnew-paper-a-roadmap-for-a-global-asset-registry-measuring-and-tackling-inequality-curbing-tax-avoidance-tax-evasion-corruption-and-illicit-financial-flows.

ICRICT, 2022, 'It is time for a global asset registry to tackle hidden wealth', *ICRICT*, https://www.icrict.com/it-is-time-for-a-global-asset-registry-to-tackle-hidden-wealth.

IMF, 2019, 'Past IMF staff assessments on Offshore Financial Centers (OFCs)', *IMF.org*, https://www.imf.org/external/NP/ofca/OFCA.aspx (accessed 28.3.2023).

Internal Revenue Service, 2005, 'KPMG to pay $456 million fine for criminal violations in relation to largest ever tax shelter fraud case', *IRS News Release* IR-05-083, https://www.irs.gov/pub/irs-news/ir-05-083.pdf.

Isbell, T., 2022, 'Footing the bill? Less legitimacy, more avoidance mark African views on taxation', *Afrobarometer Policy Paper* 78.

Janský, P., Meinzer, M., & Palanský, M., 2022, 'Is Panama really your tax haven? Secrecy jurisdictions and the countries they harm', *Regulation and Governance* 16(3), 673–704.

Joshi, P., 2020, 'Does private country-by-country reporting deter tax avoidance and income shifting? Evidence from BEPS Action Item 13', *Journal of Accounting Research* 58(2), 333–381.

Khadjavi, M., & Vertelman, M., 2022, 'Closing Pandora's box: How to improve the common reporting standard', *IfW Kiel Working Paper* 2223.

Knobel, A., 2019a, *Beneficial Ownership Verification: Ensuring the Truthfulness and Accuracy of Registered Ownership Information*, London: Tax Justice Network/Financial Transparency Coalition, https://taxjustice.net/reports/beneficial-ownership-verification-ensuring-the-truthfulness-and-accuracy-of-registered-ownership-information/ (accessed 28.3.2023).

Knobel, A., 2019b, 'Pilot study for a UK Asset Registry – Phase 1: An assessment of available asset ownership information', *ICRICT*, https://www.icrict.com/press-release/2019/12/19/icricts-study-of-asset-ownership-information-available-in-the-uk-a-stepping-stone-towards-a-global-asset-registry.

Knobel., A., 2020a, 'Germany's new statistics on exchange of banking information: A trove of useful data and clues', *Tax Justice Network* (21 August), https://taxjustice.net/2020/08/21/germanys-new-statistics-on-exchange-of-banking-information-a-trove-of-useful-data-and-clues/.

Knobel, A., 2020b, 'Developing countries, take note: How much money do your residents hold in Australia, the most transparent country on bank account information', *Tax Justice Network* (10 August), https://taxjustice.net/2020/08/10/developing-countries-take-note-how-much-money-do-your-residents-hold-in-australia-the-most-transparent-country-on-bank-account-information/.

Knobel, A., & Meinzer, M., 2017, 'Delivering a level playing field for offshore bank accounts: What the new OECD/Global Forum peer reviews on automatic information exchange must not miss', London: Tax Justice Network/Financial Transparency Coalition, https://taxjustice.net/wp-content/uploads/2013/04/TJN_AIE_ToR_Mar-1-2017.pdf (accessed 28.3.2023).

Langenmayr, D., & Zyska, L., 2023, 'Escaping the exchange of information: Tax evasion via citizenship-by-investment', *Journal of Public Economics* 221, 104865.

Lawrence, F., & Griffiths, I., 2007, 'Revealed: How multinational companies avoid the taxman', *The Guardian* (6 November), https://www.theguardian.com/business/2007/nov/06/19 (accessed 28.3.2023).

Leigh, D., Ball, J., Garside, J., Pegg, D., 2015, 'HSBC files show how Swiss bank helped clients dodge taxes and hide millions', *The Guardian* (8 February), https://www.theguardian.com/business/2015/feb/08/hsbc-files-expose-swiss-bank-clients-dodge-taxes-hide-millions.

Levi, M., 1988, *Of Rule and Revenue*, Berkeley, CA: University of California Press.

Lin, W., 2021, 'Giving too much and paying too little? The effect of corporate social responsibility on corporate lobbying efficacy: Evidence of tax aggressiveness', *Corporate Social Responsibility and Environmental Management* 28(2), 908–924.

Lorde, A., 1984, 'The Master's Tools Will Never Dismantle the Master's House', pp. 110–114 in Audre Lorde, *Sister Outsider: Essays and Speeches*, Berkeley, CA: Crossing Press.

Luxembourg, 2021, 'LuxLetters: Statement by the Luxembourg Government on press articles published about tax rulings and so-called information letters', 4 July, https://gouvernement.lu/en/dossiers/2021/luxletters.html (accessed 28.3.2023).

Maclean, N., 2017, *Democracy in Chains: The Deep History of the Radical Right's Stealth Plan for America*, New York: Viking Press.

Mager, F., & Chaparro, S., 2023, 'Delivering climate justice using the principles of tax justice', *Tax Justice Network position paper*, https://taxjustice.net/wp-content/uploads/2023/06/Policy-brief-climate-justice_2206.pdf (accessed 12.8.2023).

Marmot, M., Allen, J., Boyce, T., Goldblatt, P., & Morrison, J., 2020, *Health Equity in England: The Marmot Review 10 Years on*, London: Institute of Health Equity.

Martin, I., Mehrotra, A., & Prasad, M., 2009, 'The thunder of history: The origins and development of the new fiscal sociology', in I. Martin, A. Mehrotra, & M. Prasad (eds.), *The New Fiscal Sociology: Taxation in comparative and historical perspective*, Cambridge: Cambridge University Press, cited in Bhambra (2022).

Meade, J., & Li, S., 2015, 'Strategic corporate tax lobbying', *Journal of the American Taxation Association* 37(2), 23–48.

Meinzer, M., 2012, *The Creeping Futility of the Global Forum's Peer Reviews*, London: Tax Justice Network, http://www.taxjustice.net/cms/upload/GlobalForum2012-TJN-Briefing.pdf (accessed 12.8.2023).

Mischon de Reya, 2022, 'European Court of Justice strikes down public registers of beneficial ownership', https://www.mishcon.com/news/european-court-of-justice-strikes-down-public-registers-of-beneficial-ownership (accessed 28.3.2023).

Morris, J., Schlepper, L., Dayan, M., Jefferies, D., Maguire, D., Merry, L., & Wellings, D., 2023, *Public Satisfaction with the NHS and Social Care in 2022: Results from the British Social Attitudes Survey*, London: King's Fund & Nuffield Foundation.

Morris, M., 2017, 'The 26 OECD common reporting standard loopholes', https://www.academia.edu/download/89029479/oecd-crs-loopholes-report.pdf.

Murphy, R., 2003, *A Proposed International Accounting Standard: Reporting Turnover and Tax by Location*, Essex: Association for Accountancy and Business Affairs.

NBC, 2019, 'Google pays France over $1 billion to settle tax case', 12 September, https://www.nbcnews.com/tech/tech-news/google-pays-france-over-1-billion-settle-tax-case-n1053106 (accessed 12.8.2023).

Ndikumana, L., & Boyce, J., 1998, 'Congo's odious debt: External borrowing and capital flight in Zaire', *Development and Change* 29(2), 195–217.

Ndikumana, L., & Boyce, J., 2003, 'Public debts and private assets: Explaining capital flight from sub-Saharan African countries', *World Development* 31(1), 107–30.

Ndikumana, L., & Boyce, J., 2010, 'Measurement of capital flight: Methodology and results for sub-Saharan African countries', *African Development Review* 22(4), 471–81.

Ndikumana, L., & Boyce, J., 2011a, 'Capital flight from sub-Saharan Africa: Linkages with external borrowing and policy options', *International Review of Applied Economics* 25(2), 149–70.

Ndikumana, L., & Boyce, J., 2011b, *Africa's Odious Debts: How Foreign Loans and Capital Flight Bled a Continent*, London: Zed Books.

Ndikumana, L., & Boyce, J., 2018, 'Capital flight from Africa: Updated methodology and new estimates', *PERI Research Report*, https://peri.umass.edu/publication/item/1083-capital-flight-from-africa-updated-methodology-and-new-estimates (accessed 28.3.2023).

Nelson, L., 2021, *Tax Justice & Human Rights: The 4 Rs and the Realisation of Rights*, London: Tax Justice Network, https://taxjustice.net/reports/tax-justice-human-rights-the-4-rs-and-the-realisation-of-rights/.

Noked, N., 2018, 'Tax evasion and incomplete tax transparency', *Laws* 7(3), 31, https://doi.org/10.3390/laws7030031.

OCCRP, 2014, *The Russian Laundromat*, https://www.occrp.org/en/russianlaundromat/ (accessed 12.8.2023).

OCCRP, & Süddeutsche Zeitung, 2022, 'Historic leak of Swiss banking records reveals unsavory clients', *OCCRP.org* (20 Feburary), https://www.occrp.org/

en/suisse-secrets/historic-leak-of-swiss-banking-records-reveals-unsavory-clients (accessed 28.3.2023).

OECD, 2000, 'Improving access to bank information for tax purposes', *OECD Committee on Fiscal Affairs Report*, Paris: Organisation for Economic Co-operation and Development.

OECD, 2022, *Global Revenue Statistics Database*, https://www.datawrapper.de/_/W6mi3/ (accessed 4.8.2023).

Ogle, V., 2020, '"Funk money": The end of empires, the expansion of tax havens, and decolonization as an economic and financial event', *Past and Present* 249(1), 213–249.

O'Hare, B., Lopez, M., Mazimbe, B., Murray, S., Spencer, N., Torrie, C., & Hall, S., 2022, 'Tax abuse—The potential for the Sustainable Development Goals', *PLOS Global Public Health* 2(2).

On behalf of WM, 2020, 'Summary of the request for a preliminary ruling pursuant to Article 98(1) of the Rules of Procedure of the Court of Justice', *European Court of Justice* case C-37/20.

OUCBT, 2023, 'What is the Centre for Business Taxation?', https://oxfordtax.sbs.ox.ac.uk/about-us (accessed 12.8.2023).

Overesch, M., & Wolff, H., 2021, 'Financial transparency to the rescue: Effects of public country-by-country reporting in the European Union banking sector on tax avoidance', *Contemporary Accounting Research* 38(3), 1616–1642.

Oxfam, 2000, 'Tax Havens: Releasing the hidden billions for poverty eradication', *Briefing Paper* (June).

Palan, R., 2002, 'Tax havens and the commercialization of state sovereignty', *International Organization* 56, 151–176.

Palan, R., Murphy, R., & Chavagneux, C., 2010, *Tax Havens: How Globalization Really Works*, Ithaca, NY: Cornell University Press.

Peco, D., Tsogoeva, A., Baquero, B., Stocks, T., Caregari, L., & Huppertz, C., 2023, 'This Luxembourg businessman got Europe's corporate registries shut down. But whose privacy was he protecting?', *OCCRP.org* (10 February), https://www.occrp.org/en/beneficial-ownership-data-is-critical-in-the-fight-against-corruption/this-luxembourg-businessman-got-europes-corporate-registries-shut-down-but-whose-privacy-was-he-protecting (accessed 28.3.2023).

Pegg, D., Makortoff, K., Chulov, M., Lewis, P., & Harding, L., 2022, 'Revealed: Credit Suisse leak unmasks criminals, fraudsters and corrupt politicians', *The Guardian* (20 February), https://www.theguardian.com/news/2022/feb/20/credit-suisse-secrets-leak-unmasks-criminals-fraudsters-corrupt-politicians.

Picciotto, S., 1992, *International Business Taxation: A Study in the Internationalization of Business Regulation*, Cambridge: Cambridge University

Press, now published in open access at https://www.taxjustice.net/cms/ upload/pdf/Picciotto%201992%20International%20Business%20Taxation.pdf (accessed 28.3.2023).

Picciotto, S., 2012, *Towards Unitary Taxation*, London: Tax Justice Network, https://www.taxjustice.net/cms/upload/pdf/Towards_Unitary_Taxation_1-1.pdf (accessed 12.8.2023).

Picciotto, S. (ed.), 2017, *Taxing Multinational Enterprises as Unitary Firms*, Brighton: International Centre for Tax and Development, https://www.ictd.ac/ publication/taxing-multinational-enterprises-as-unitary-firms-2/ (accessed 12.8.2023).

Picciotto, S., Ahmed, A., Cobham, A., Das, R., Eze, E., & Michel, B., 2023 (forthcoming), 'Beyond the Two Pillar Proposals: A simplified approach for taxing multinationals', *South Centre Tax Cooperation Policy Brief*.

Piketty, T., 2014, *Capital in the Twenty-First Century*, Cambridge, MA: Harvard University Press.

Pistor, K., 2019, *The Code of Capital: How the Law Creates Wealth and Inequality*, Princeton, NJ: Princeton University Press.

Prichard, W., Cobham, A., & Goodall, A, 2014, 'The ICTD Government Revenue Dataset', *International Centre for Tax and Development Working Paper* 19, https://www.ictd.ac/publication/the-ictd-government-revenue-dataset/ (accessed 12.8.2023).

Prichard, W., Salardi, P., & Segal, P., 2018, 'Taxation, non-tax revenue and democracy: New evidence using new cross-country data', *World Development* 109, 295–312.

Quentin, C., 2017, 'Risk-mining the public exchequer', *Journal of Tax Administration* 3(2), 22–35, http://jota.website/index.php/JoTA/article/ view/142/118.

Quentin, C., 2019, 'Acceptable levels of tax risk as a metric of corporate tax responsibility: Theory, and a survey of practice', *Nordic Tax Journal* (1): 1–15, https://doi.org/10.1515/ntaxj-2019-0001.

Quiñones, N., 2023, 'Policy Note: Beyond the 2-Pillar solution: A case for a global income tax and the creation of the international tax organization', *Intertax* 51(4), 324–334.

Reagan, R, 1989, *Farewell Address to the Nation*, https://www.reaganfoundation. org/media/128655/farewell.pdf (accessed 12.8.2023).

Reeves, A., Gourtsoyannis, Y., Basu, S., McCoy, D., McKee, M., & Stuckler, D., 2015, 'Financing universal health coverage. Effects of alternative tax structures on public health systems: Cross-national modelling in 89 low-income and middle-income countries', *The Lancet* 386(9990), 274–280.

Reitz, F., 2023, 'Revenue effects of the OECD corporate tax reform – An updated impact assessment of Pillar Two', *Universität St. Gallen IFF-HSG Working Papers* 2023-17.

Richter, B., Samphantharak, K., & Timmons, J., 2009, 'Lobbying and taxes', *American Journal of Political Science* 53(4), 893–909.

Rodney, W., 2018 (1972), *How Europe Underdeveloped Africa*, London: Verso.

Rubin, P., 1977, 'Why is the common law efficient?', *Journal of Legal Studies* 6(1), 51–63.

Russ, K., Baker, P., Kang, M., & McCoy, D.,'2022, 'Corporate lobbying on US positions toward the World Health Organization: Evidence of intensification and cross-industry coordination', *Global Health Governance* XVII(1), 37–83.

Ryding, T., 2022, *Proposal for a United Nations Convention on Tax*, Eurodad/ Global Alliance for Tax Justice, https://globaltaxjustice.org/news/ground-breaking-civil-society-proposal-for-a-un-convention-on-tax-is-published/ (accessed 28.3.2023).

Sævold, K., 2022, 'Tax havens of the British Empire: Development, policy responses, and decolonization, 1961–1979', *PhD thesis*, Bergen: University of Bergen.

Savoia, A., Sen, K., & Tagem, A., 2023, 'Constraints on the executive and tax revenues in the long run', *Journal of Institutional Economics* 19, 314–331.

Scottish Government, 2021, *Framework for Tax*, Edinburgh: Scottish Government, https://www.gov.scot/publications/framework-tax-2021/ (accessed 4.8.2023).

Shaxson, N., 2011, *Treasure Islands. Tax Havens and the Men Who Stole the World*, London: Bodley Head.

Sheppard, L., 2009, 'Don't ask, don't tell, part 4: Ineffectual information sharing', *Tax Notes* (23 March), 1411–1418.

Siahaan, F., 2013, 'The effect of tax transparency and trust on taxpayers' voluntary compliance', *GSTF Journal on Business Review* 2(3).

Siddique, H., & Davies, H., 2022, 'Top UK law firm fined record sum for breaching money-laundering rules', *The Guardian* (6 January), https://www.theguardian.com/law/2022/jan/06/top-uk-law-firm-fined-record-sum-serious-money-laundering-rule-breaches-mishcon-de-reya (accessed 29.3.2023).

Slobodian, Q., 2020, *Globalists: The End of Empire and the Birth of Neoliberalism*, Cambridge, MA: Harvard University Press.

Slobodian, Q., 2023, *Crack-Up Capitalism: Market Radicals and the Dream of a World Without Democracy*, London: Allen Lane.

Smith, A., 1776, *The Wealth of Nations*, https://en.wikisource.org/wiki/The_Wealth_of_Nations/ (accessed 12.8.2023).

Smith, K., Savell, E., & Gilmore, A., 2013, 'What is known about tobacco industry efforts to influence tobacco tax? A systematic review of empirical studies', *Tobacco Control* 22(1).

Snyckers, T., 2020, *Dirty Tobacco: Spies, Lies and Mega-Profits*, Cape Town: Tafelberg.

Tanzi, V., 1999, 'Is there a need for a world tax organization?', pp. 173–186 in A, Razin & E. Sadka (eds.), *The Economics of Globalization: Perspectives from Public Economics*, Cambridge: Cambridge University Press.

Tax Justice Network, 2005a, *Tax Us If You Can*, London: Tax Justice Network.

Tax Justice Network, 2005b, *The Price of Offshore*, London: Tax Justice Network, https://taxjustice.net/cms/upload/pdf/Price_of_Offshore.pdf.

Tax Justice Network, 2007, 'Tax Justice Goes Bananas', https://taxjustice. blogspot.com/2007/11/tax-justice-goes-bananas.html (accessed 28.3.2023).

Tax Justice Network, 2015, *Ten Reasons to Defend the Corporation Tax: How the corporate income tax protects democracy and curbs inequality... and seven myths, busted*, London: Tax Justice Network, https://taxjustice.net/ wp-content/uploads/2013/04/Ten_Reasons_Full_Report.pdf (accessed 12.8.2023).

Tax Justice Network, 2017, 'Campaign victory disarms big tobacco's lobby front in developing countries', https://www.taxjustice.net/2017/05/22/campaign-victory-disarms-big-tobaccos-lobby-front-developing-countries/ (accessed 12.8.2023).

Tax Justice Network, 2020, 'Investors demand OECD tax transparency', 19 March, https://taxjustice.net/2020/03/19/investors-demand-oecd-tax-transparency/ (accessed 12.8.2023).

Tax Justice Network, 2021, *State of Tax Justice 2021*, Bristol: Tax Justice Network.

Tax Justice Network, 2022, *Secrecy Indicator 14: Tax Court Rulings*, https://fsi. taxjustice.net/fsi2022/KFSI-14.pdf (accessed 28.3.2023).

Tax Justice Network, 2023, *State of Tax Justice 2023*, Bristol: Tax Justice Network.

Tax Justice UK, 2023, 'How much tax does the Prime Minister pay?', 23 March, https://www.taxjustice.uk/blog/how-much-tax-does-the-prime-minister-pay (accessed 28.3.2023).

Tietjen, B., 2022, 'Loss and damage: Who is responsible when climate change harms the world's poorest countries?', *The Conversation* (2 November), https://theconversation.com/loss-and-damage-who-is-responsible-when-climate-change-harms-the-worlds-poorest-countries-192070 (accessed 4.8.2023).

Tobacconomics & STOP, 2023, *Tobacco Taxes Promote Equity: Evidence from Around the Globe*, https://www.tobacconomics.org/research/tobacco-taxes-promote-equity-evidence-from-around-the-globe/ (accessed 12.10.2023).

Tørsløv, T., Wier, L., & Zucman, G., 2023, `The missing profits of nations', *Review of Economic Studies* 90(3), 1499-1534.

Ülgen, S., 2023, 'A political economy perspective on the EU's carbon border tax', *Carnegie Europe* (9 May), https://carnegieeurope.eu/2023/05/09/political-economy-perspective-on-eu-s-carbon-border-tax-pub-89706 (accessed 12.8.2023).

UNICEF, 2023, *Levels and Trends in Child Mortality Report 2022: Estimates developed by the United Nations Inter-agency Group for Child Mortality Estimation*, New York: United Nations.

UNODC & UNCTAD, 2020, *Conceptual Framework for the Statistical Measurement of Illicit Financial Flows*, Vienna: United Nations Office on Drugs and Crime.

US Congress, 1939, Hearings: Volume 2, p. 449: https://www.google.fr/books/edition/Hearings/RjwhFw9RPqYC?hl=en&gbpv=1&dq=%22tax+justice%22&pg=RA9-PA449&printsec=frontcover (accessed 14/9/22).

US Congress, 1969, Hearings: Ninety-First Congress, p. 915: https://www.google.fr/books/edition/Tax_Reform_Act_of_1969/vEJKAQAAIAAJ?hl=en&gbpv=1&dq=%22tax+justice%22&pg=PA915&printsec=frontcover (accessed 14/9/22).

US Senate Finance Committee, 2023, 'Credit Suisse's role in US tax evasion schemes', *Democratic Staff Investigation* (29 March), https://www.finance.senate.gov/imo/media/doc/SFC%20CREDIT%20SUISSE%20REPORT%20FINAL%20Mar%2028.pdf (accessed 29.3.2023).

Vaughan, M., 2019, 'Mobilisation for international tax justice after the financial crisis in the UK and Australia', *DPhil. Thesis*, University of Sydney, https://ses.library.usyd.edu.au/handle/2123/21292 (accessed 28.3.2023).

Viegas, M., & Dias, A., 2021, 'Country-by-country reporting: A step towards unitary taxation?', *Intereconomics* 56, 167–173, https://doi.org/10.1007/s10272-021-0974-9 (accessed 28.3.2023).

Washington State Budget & Policy Center, 2022, 'Press release: Capital gains tax is constitutional, and needed, say tax law experts and advocates: Amicus briefs filed today ahead of January state Supreme Court hearing on child care funding', 12 December, https://budgetandpolicy.org/schmudget/press-release-capital-gains-tax-is-constitutional-and-needed-say-tax-law-experts-and-advocates/ (accessed 12.8.2023).

Wier, L., & Zucman, G., 2022, 'Global profit shifting, 1975–2019', *WIDER Working Paper* 2022/121, https://doi.org/10.35188/UNU-WIDER/2022/254-6.

Wightman, A., 2010, *The Poor Had No Lawyers: Who Owns Scotland and How They Got It*, Edinburgh: Birlinn.

Williamson, J., 1990, 'What Washington means by policy reform', ch. 2 in J. Williamson (ed.), *Latin American Adjustment: How Much Has Happened?*, Washington, DC: Institute for International Economics: https://piie.com/commentary/speeches-papers/what-washington-means-policy-reform (accessed 28.3.2023).

WilmerHale, 2021, 'Investigation of Data Irregularities in *Doing Business 2018* and *Doing Business 2020*: Investigation findings and report to the board of executive directors', Washington, DC: World Bank, https://thedocs.worldbank.org/en/doc/84a922cc9273b7b120d49ad3b9e9d3f9-0090012021/original/DB-Investigation-Findings-and-Report-to-the-Board-of-Executive-Directors-September-15-2021.pdf (accessed 12.8.2023).

Woodman, S., 'HSBC moved vast sums of dirty money after paying record laundering fine', *ICIJ.org* (21.9.2020), https://www.icij.org/investigations/fincen-files/hsbc-moved-vast-sums-of-dirty-money-after-paying-record-laundering-fine/.

World Bank, 2022, *Correcting Course: Poverty and Shared Prosperity 2022*, Washington, DC: World Bank.

Zatoński, M., Egbe, C., Robertson, L., & Gilmore, A., 2023, 'Framing the policy debate over tobacco control legislation and tobacco taxation in South Africa´, *Tobacco Control* 32, 450–457.

Zucman, G., 2013, 'The missing wealth of nations: Are Europe and the US net debtors or net creditors?', *The Quarterly Journal of Economics* 128(3), 1321–64.

Zucman, G., 2014, 'Taxing across borders: Tracking personal wealth and corporate profits', *Journal of Economic Perspectives* 28(4), 121–148.

Zucman, G., 2015, *The Hidden Wealth of Nations*, Chicago: Chicago University Press.

Zuluaga, D., 2016, 'Let's abolish corporation tax', *Institute for Economic Affairs blog*, https://iea.org.uk/blog/lets-abolish-corporation-tax (accessed 12.8.2023).

index

Abbott Laboratories, 54
ABC of tax transparency, 72–88
  automatic exchange of information,
    72–78
  beneficial ownership transparency,
    78–83
  country by county reporting, 83–88
accountability, 9, 83, 89, 92–93, 113
ActionAid, 35, 110
Advance Rulings Commission, 55
Afrobarometer, 11
anomalies, 46, 47
anonymous ownership, ending, 78–83
arm's length pricing, 56, 103–106
audit rates, 95
austerity, 95
  arguments, 5
authority disclosures, 89
automatic exchange of information, on
  financial accounts, 72–78
'axis of avoidance,' 50, 53, 61, 62

Bank for International Settlements,
  47–48, 93
bank secrecy, ending, 72–78
beneficial ownership transparency,
  78–83
BEPS (Base Erosion and Profit Shifting)
  process, 59, 104–105
Bilicka, Katarzyna, 57
Blair, Tony, 73
Boston Consulting Group, 49
Boyce, J., 46, 47, 69
Brown, Dorothy, 32, 91
Brown, Gordon, 73, 74

Cameron, David, 79
Capital in the Twenty-First Century
  (2014), 102
carbon emissions, reduction of, 100–101
certainty and convenience, 21
Chancel, Lucas, 100
Chege, Kamau, 31
Christian Aid, 110
Civil Society Group on Financing for
  Development, 111
Common Reporting Standard (CRS),
  73–78, 93
corporate disclosures, 89, 92
corporate tax, 12, 34, 53, 54, 58
  abuse, 41, 50, 53, 57, 60–61, 64, 68,
    84, 85, 93, 102, 110
  revenues, 58, 59, 64
Corporate Tax Haven Index (CTHI), 61,
  62, 92
cost-benefit analysis, 92
country by county reporting, 83–88
*Crack-Up Capitalism: Market Radicals
  and the Dream of a World Without
  Democracy* (2023), 10
Credit Suisse, 44–45, 55
Credit Suisse Global Wealth Report
  (2011), 48
cross-border deposits, 48–50, 93
cross-border tax abuse, 32–35, 36, 42,
  53, 63, 69, 70, 110
Crown Dependencies, 50, 52

Davis, Mike, 65
De Reya, Mishcon, 81
Decolonising Economics, 91

disclosures, 88–94
domestic measures
  disclosures, 88–94
  enforcement, 94–99
  good taxes, 99–101
double tax treaties, 41

ECORYS, 49–50, 77
efficiency, 21
enforcement, 94–99
engagement, 22
EU, 38, 55–56, 74, 80–82, 85, 87, 105
Eurodad, 107
European Commission, 54
European Federation of Public Services
  Unions (EPSU), 94

Fair Tax Foundation, 85, 86
Fairness Foundation, 10
Falciani, Hervé, 43
finance curse, 7
Financial Accounting Standards Board,
  US, 87
Financial Action Task Force (FATF),
  78, 82
financial crisis, 5, 73, 89, 95, 110–111
financial secrecy
  jurisdictions, 34
  risks of, 68
Financial Secrecy Index, 51, 52, 61,
  92, 96
Foreign Account Tax Compliance Act
  (FATCA), 74
formulary apportionment, 104
4 Rs of tax, 3–10, 22, 64
Framework for Tax, 21, 22, 23
frauds, 40–41, 44
Freedman, Judith, 39
funk money, 66

G20 group of countries, 60, 74,
  84, 104
G-24 group of countries, 105, 106
G77 group of countries, 107, 110
Garcia-Bernardo, Javier, 59

Global Alliance for Tax Justice, 35,
  107, 111
global asset registry (GAR), 102–103
Global Financial Integrity, 47
Global Forum, 78
global governance, 106–108
Global Reporting Initiative (GRI)
  standards, 86, 92
Global Tax Expenditures Database, 92
global tax revenue loss, 49
globalisation, 73
golden visas, 76
good taxes, 99–101
Google, 40–41
Government Accountability Office, 95
GRADE model (Government Revenue
  and Development Estimations), 4–5
gross domestic product (GDP), 19
The Guardian newspaper, 44, 54

Hakelberg, Lukas, 77
harms and history, 63–70
haven score, 61–62
Henry, James, 46, 47–48, 49
High-Level Panel on Illicit Financial
  Flows out of Africa, 97, 109–110
HMRC (His Majesty's Revenue and
  Customs), 21, 38, 73
Hobbes, Thomas, 1, 21
HSBC, 42–45
The Hypocritical Hegemon (2020), 77

illicit financial flows, 16, 36, 64–65, 69,
  97–98, 110, 113
Improving Access to Bank Information
  for Tax Purposes (OECD
  study), 73
Independent Commission for the Reform
  of International Corporate
  Taxation, 102
inequalities, 32, 64, 91, 99–101
'Information Letter,' 55
Institute of Business Ethics, 53
Instituto Justiça Fiscal (Brazil), 35
Internal Revenue Service, of US, 78

international and institutional measures, 102–108
  arm's length pricing to unitary taxation, 103–106
  global asset registry (GAR), 102–103
  global governance, 106–108
International Consortium of Investigative Journalists, 54
International Monetary Fund (IMF), 12, 22, 64, 94
investors, 41, 86–87

Janský, Petr, 59
Juncker, Jean-Claude, 54
jurisdictions
  financial secrecy, 34
  positive/negative relationships between, 41–42

King's Fund, 5
KPMG, 41
kryptonite, 15

Le Monde newspaper, 43
League of Nations, 56, 103
leaks and legal cases, 42–46
Levi, Margaret, 20–21
Levi's theory of predatory rule, 21
lobbying, 6, 15
Lorde, Audre, 36
lower-income countries, 8, 24, 61, 63, 69, 73, 75–76, 88, 100, 105–107
Luttgrodt, Marta, 35
LuxLeaks, 54, 92
LuxLetters, 55, 92

Major, John, 24
The Master's Tools Will Never Dismantle the Master's House (1984, essay), 36
Mbeki, Thabo, 109
McKinsey's, 12
Millennium Development Goals (MDGs), 109
monetary fines, 43

Mossack Fonseca, 45
multinationals
  country by county reporting by, 83–88
  tax abuse, 53–63

National Committee for Tax Justice, 29
National Health Service (NHS), 2
Ndikumana, L., 46, 47, 69
neoliberalism, 32–35
neutrality, of tax system, 23

Obama, Barack, 74
OCCRP, 79
offshore banking centres, 67
offshore tax evasion, 41, 42–53, 68, 93
Ogle, Vanessa, 66
Organisation for Economic Cooperation and Development (OECD) countries, 17, 20, 50, 53, 61, 62–63, 73–76, 84–88, 106–107, 111
Oxfam, 73, 110
Oxford University Centre for Business Taxation, 48

Panama Papers, 45
Pandora Papers, 46
Paying Taxes, 48
performance outcome areas (POAs), 94
Piketty, Thomas, 102
policymakers, 13
political representation, 8–10, 22
profit shifting, 16, 17, 27, 41, 42, 56, 59–60, 67, 93, 105–106
proportionality, 21
public attitudes and media coverage, 53–57
public health, 2
  spending, 3, 9
Public Services International, 111
PwC, 39–40, 48, 54

Reagan, Ronald, 10, 33, 111
Red de Justicia Fiscal de América Latina y el Caribe, 35
redistribution, 6, 22

registers, 79–81
reparative/restorative justice, 70
representation, political, 8–10, 22
repricing, of public goods and bads,
6–8, 22
revenues, 4–5, 22

SABMiller, 35
Sævold, Kristine, 67
scale weight, 51, 61–62
secrecy score, 51
Shaxson, Nicholas, 67
Sheppard, Lee, 74
Signals Network, 55
Slobodian, Quinn, 10
Smith, Adam, 21
spider's web, UK, 50, 52–53, 61, 62,
68, 70
SSE company, 85
State of Tax Justice, 2, 50, 60–61,
63, 105
Süddeutsche Zeitung newspaper, 45
Suisse Secrets, 44, 76
Sunak, Rishi, 30
Sustainable Development Goals (SDGs),
109, 110
Swiss Leaks, 43

Tanzi, Vito, 106
tax(es), 2
  abuse, 2, 4, 6, 17, 32–39
  administration, 96
  avoidance, 38–39, 40
  consensus, 23–24
  direct/indirect, 19, 20, 38, 99
  enforcement, 94
  evasion, 38–39, 41, 42–53
  4 Rs of, 3–10, 22, 64
  global governance of, 106–108
  good, 99–101
  havens, 27–28, 34, 49, 56, 58–59, 66,
  67, 73
  losses, 2–3
  paying, 14, 24
  rates on labour and capital, 30, 31

revenues, 19–20
  as social superpower, 10–15
  VAT, 9, 13, 20
  see also specific entries
Tax Administration Diagnostic
  Assessment Tool (TADAT), 94
Tax and Fiscal Justice Asia, 35
Tax Cuts and Jobs Act, 59
Tax Information Exchange Agreements
  (TIEAs), 74
tax justice
  A to G of, 112
  challenging cross-border tax abuse,
  32–35
  domestic focus, equal tax rates,
  28–32
  global and reparative demand, 35–37
  organisations, 35
  perspectives on, 28–37
  scale of, 37
Tax Justice-Europe, 35
Tax Justice Network (TJN), 3, 12, 33, 46,
  51, 55, 61, 72, 84, 87, 97, 107
Tax Justice Network-Africa, 35
Tax Justice Network-Australia, 35
Tax Justice Norge (Norway), 35
tax-washing, 49
Thatcher, Margaret, 24, 33, 67
tobacco taxation, 7
Tørsløv, Thomas, 58
transfer pricing, 56, 57

UBS, 45
UK
  Fair Tax Foundation, 85, 86
  income tax position for households,
  89–90
  National Health Service (NHS), 2
  outward banking positions, 98
  spider's web, 50, 52–53, 61, 62,
  68, 70
  tax revenues, 67
  10-year Tax Administration
  Strategy, 21
unitary taxation, 103–106

United Nations, 36, 83
  Financing Sustainable Development
    Report, 76
  General Assembly, 107
  Millennium Development Goals
    (MDGs), 109
  University's World Institute for
    Development Economics
    Research (UNU-WIDER), 9
US Senate Finance Committee, 45

VAT (value-added tax), 9, 13, 20
verification and validation, of public
    beneficial ownership data, 80
Vodafone, 54, 84

vulnerability, to illicit financial flows,
    97–98

Washington Community Alliance, 31
Washington Consensus,
    22, 23
'web of generalised reciprocity,'
    15, 25
The Whiteness of Wealth
    (2021), 32
Wier, Ludwig, 58
Williamson, John, 22
World Bank, 19, 48, 63

Zucman, Gabriel, 46, 58, 102